IMAGES
of America

COPIAGUE

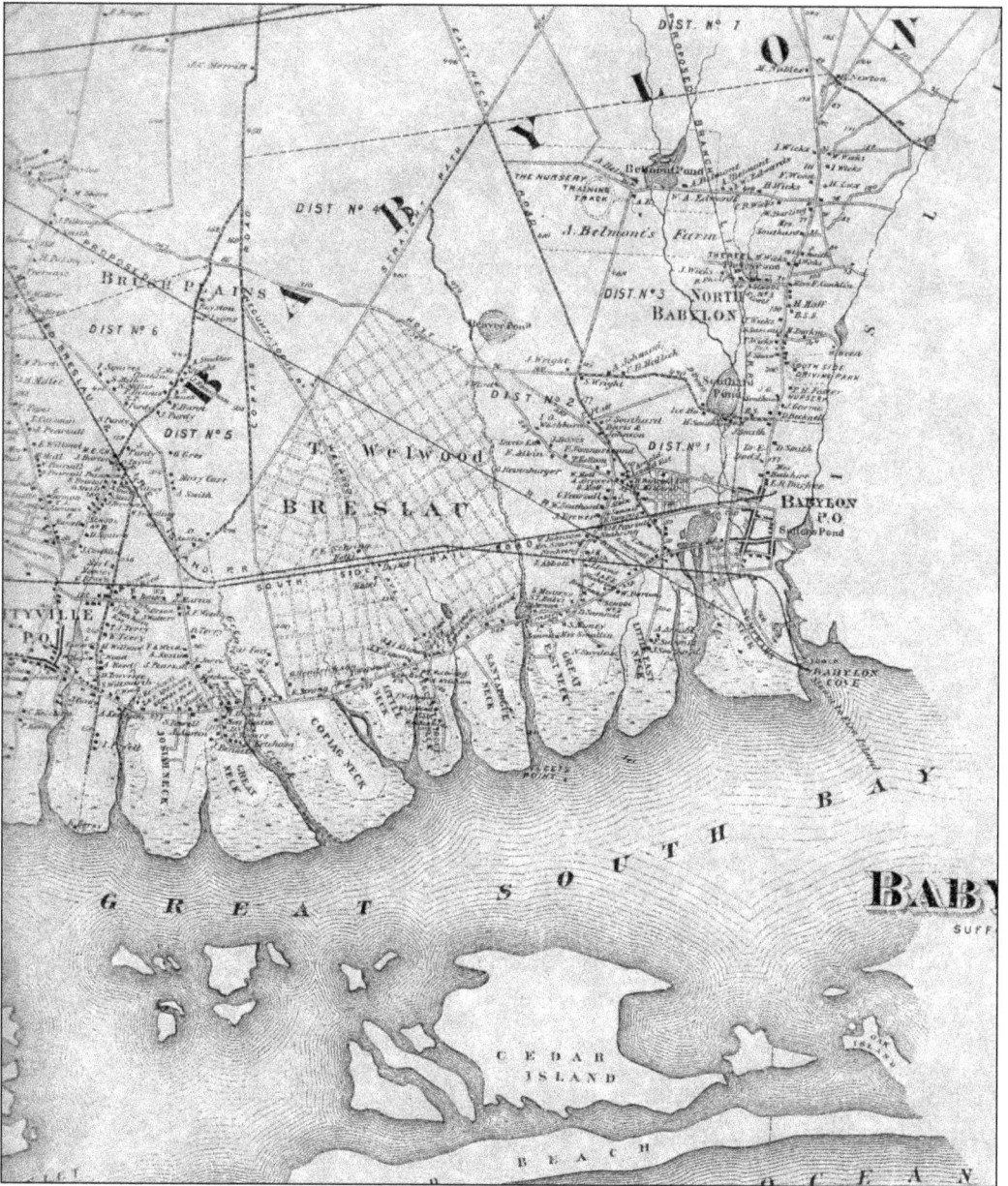

The hamlet of Copiague is one of 10 unincorporated communities in the town of Babylon. This 1873 map of the town of Babylon (published in the *Atlas of Long Island, New York*, by Beers, Comstock, and Cline) details its 11 natural necks or peninsulas, named from left to right, West, Josiah's, Half, Great, Copiague, Little, Neguntatogue, Santapogue, Great East, Little East, and Sumpwams. Situated between the two incorporated villages of Amityville and Lindenhurst, Copiague extends from the south shore necks of Half Neck, Great Neck, and Copiague Neck to north of present-day Sunrise Highway. (Courtesy of the History Collections, Office of Historic Services, Town of Babylon.)

ON THE COVER: The Copiague Fire Department parades down Great Neck Road about 1957. (Courtesy of Veterans of Foreign Wars, Warren Keer Post No. 9483, Copiague, New York.)

IMAGES
of America

COPIAGUE

Mary Cascone

ARCADIA
PUBLISHING

Copyright © 2010 by Mary Cascone
ISBN 978-1-5316-4815-2

Published by Arcadia Publishing
Charleston, South Carolina

Library of Congress Control Number: 2010920200

For all general information contact Arcadia Publishing at:
Telephone 843-853-2070
Fax 843-853-0044
E-mail sales@arcadiapublishing.com
For customer service and orders:
Toll-Free 1-888-313-2665

Visit us on the Internet at www.arcadiapublishing.com

For Jason and Benjamin, with love and devotion, and for our fellow Copiagueions, whose inspiration made this book a reality.

CONTENTS

FOREWORD

History is important. It is through an understanding of our history that we become connected to both our past and the future. When we appreciate and understand our history, we recognize that we are part of a larger story. We make a connection with the people and things that have come before us and those that will follow.

Establishing a connection with our local history is most important of all. For it is in our own local communities that we spend most of our time, raise our families, forge friendships with neighbors, and join organizations to help others. Strong communities form the foundation of our great nation, and Copiague is a shining example of such a community.

The history of Copiague, as articulated through the words and photographs in this book, tells the story of a community that personifies the unique history of the United States. In Copiague, Native Americans were followed by fishermen and farmers, a rural lifestyle gave way to the suburban dream, and countless immigrants staked their futures there.

Along the way, Copiague has seen its share of visionaries and dreamers, like the men who sought to create an American Venice on the south shore of Long Island only to have that vision decimated by the Great Depression. Copiague is home to the oldest continuously operating civic association in New York and the oldest black church on Long Island. Its history includes the famous inventor Guglielmo Marconi and George Washington, the father of our country. However, it is not the famous or celebrated who have made Copiague great, it is the veterans from the VFW Post, the volunteers from the Copiague Fire Department, the members of the Kiwanis Club, and the chamber of commerce. It is the citizens of Copiague who, through their collective efforts, have given definition and meaning to the word "community."

Today Copiague is a thriving, diverse community with beautiful parks, proud traditions, and a rich history. The story of Copiague continues to unfold, and I am honored to be able to play a small role in its telling.

—Steven Bellone
Supervisor, Town of Babylon

ACKNOWLEDGMENTS

Through my research for Copiague history projects over the past few years, I have been overwhelmed by the community's desire to not only learn about its history, but to share it with others. For their generous contributions to the collection of material for this book, my sincere thanks to the following: Steven Bellone, Babylon town supervisor; Patricia Boyle Cahaney (Cahaney); the Calandrino and Natalie families (Calandrino-Natalie); Georgia Cava; Miriam Holmes Collins (Collins); Copiague Fire Department and Bill Maniaci, Vigilant Engine Company (CFD); Copiague Memorial Public Library, Kenneth S. Miller, director; Copiague Post Office, Lisa M. Vice, postmaster (CPO); Copiague School District, Charles A. Leunig, superintendent (CSD); Copiague Youth League (CYL); *Copiague Weekly* newspaper, Ralph Soluri, editor (CW); Christ Covenant Church; Debbie DeGore (DeGore); Revolta (Nancy) Biondi Enz and Karen Enz (Enz); Steve Gravano, Babylon town photographer (Gravano); Frances J. Gusmano (Gusmano); Full Gospel Christian Church (FGCC); William T. Lauder, Amityville village historian; Robert LePorte (LePorte); Hugo Mascari (Mascari); Jeannette Mazzoli Giardina (Mazzoli); Chris O'Connell (O'Connell); Theresa Pisani (Pisani); Polish Friends of Copiague (PFoC); Lorraine Valerio Prisco (Prisco); Richard Rodi (Rodi); Jessica Ruppert; Agnes Scheuermann; Thomas B. Smith, Town of Babylon historian and curator of the Suffolk Police Museum (SPM); Marie Steinbrecher (Steinbrecher); Angelo Vacca; Veterans of Foreign Wars, Warren Keer Post No. 9483, Jerry DeFranco, commander (VFW); Robert E. Wilde; Ron Ziel Collection, Queens Borough Public Library (Ziel); Zion Gospel Church (Zion Gospel); Amityville Historical Society and Lauder Museum, Seth Purdy, curator (AHS); Village of Babylon Historical and Preservation Society and Museum, Ruth Corbin, curator, and Alice Zaruka, Babylon village historian (VBHPS); Lindenhurst Historical Society and Old Village Hall Museum, Johanna Sandy, museum director, and Evelyn Mentz Ellis, Lindenhurst village historian (LHS); Huntington Historical Society and David Conklin Farmhouse Museum, Robert "Toby" Kissam, executive coordinator; and the countless others who assisted in this historic effort. Please refer to the abbreviations provided in the above list for photograph courtesy lines found throughout the text. Unless otherwise noted, all images appear courtesy of the History Collections of the Town of Babylon, Office of Historic Services.

INTRODUCTION

"America will always be great as long as it has hamlets like Copiague." These inspirational words were offered by longtime Copiague educator Walter G. O'Connell in his 1978 book of prose *The "I" in Copiague is Silent*. O'Connell further extolled the strength and character of residents living and working in this diverse community and illustrated the community's modesty by stating, "It is significant that even in the name, Copiague, the 'i' is not pronounced: it is silent!"

Though the Copiague community of the 21st century may still retain a somewhat unassuming pretense, residents are eager to celebrate the remarkable bounty of its historic legacy. Copiague, its name derived from a Native American term meaning "harbor" or "place of shelter," has historically welcomed visitors and immigrants from around the world. The tales of President Washington's visit and those of wireless inventor Guglielmo Marconi along with stories of gondolas, beaches, and open meadows have been passed from neighbor to neighbor, from one generation to the next. The early 20th century ushered an influx of Italian immigrants to Copiague, who were followed in the latter part of the century by scores of immigrants of Hispanic and Polish descent.

One can chart the growth of Copiague through its unique summer and year-round communities created throughout the 20th century, including Marconiville, American Venice, Amity Harbor, Hawkins Estate, Deauville Gardens, Shore Acres, the Ranger Homes, and Copiague Harbor. As Copiague expanded, scores of residents assumed service and leadership roles through the school district, the fire department, the library, veterans' groups, churches, and community organizations. Each of those groups helped shape Copiague into a diverse community that will continue to thrive in the 21st century and beyond.

Copiague is more than just a unique community. Locally pronounced "koh-payg," there is no other community named "Copiague" in the entire world. Variations of the name Copiague, or Copiag, include Copyag, Cuppuauge, and Kuppi-auke, according to William Wallace Tooker (1848–1917), anthropologist and pioneer scholar in Coastal Algonquian history. Huntington town records contain a 1666 deed referencing a "passel of meddow . . . being in a neck commonly called by the Indians Coppiage." European settlers labeled the Native American groups living along the south shore using terms adapted from those given to the land by the Native Americans. Present-day Seaford to Copiague was referred to as "massapeague," meaning "great water land," and the area from Copiague to Bayport was known as "secatogue," or "black meadows." Contrary to local myth, however, there was not a Native American group named Copiague.

Colonial Dutch and English settlers would later inhabit the Copiague shores. In 1653, the town of Huntington was formed, stretching from the Long Island Sound to the Great South Bay and including all of present-day Copiague and the town of Babylon. Huntington residents predominately lived along the northern shore of the town; however, the northern residents soon discovered an abundance of natural resources in and around the Great South Bay, from salt hay to a seemingly infinite array of fish and shellfish, to feed their families. Similar to English hay, harvested salt hay was a valuable commodity to the settlers. It could be used to feed livestock and to construct their homes. Many farmers earned a significant income by harvesting the natural grown hay and transporting it to markets. The southern part of the town of Huntington, which would later become the town of Babylon, was known as "Huntington South." Most of the northern settlers who traveled south for food and salt hay kept their homes in the north. The migration of residents who permanently settled in Huntington South was slow, but that eventually changed.

The southern shoreline of the town of Babylon, along the Great South Bay, is broken up by 11 necks of land, or peninsulas. Three of those necks compose the present Copiague shoreline. Huntington town records document the "Indian Deed of Three Necks, Southside," dated August 17, 1658, between Grand Sachem Wyandance and Henry Whitney of Huntington, "for the use of the whole Town of Huntington." Copiague Neck was the easternmost of the three peninsulas in that 1658 transaction that was exchanged for "twelve coats, each coat being two yards of tucking cloth, twenty pounds of powder, twenty dutch hatchets, twenty dutch howes, twenty dutch knives, ten shirts, two hundred muxes [awl blades], five pairs of handsome stockens, one good dutch hat, and a great fine looking glass." Wyandance's agent, Cheacanoe, who marked out the land, also received "one coat, seven pounds of powder, six pounds of lead, one dutch hatchet, and also seventeen shillings in wampum." Wyandance confirmed receipt of his requested payment, stating, "Received this 23 May 1659 from the inhabitants of Huntington that satisfaction and payment for the meadow I sold last to them, which my man Cheacanoe marked out for them, which joins to that neck that [land] belongs to Mr. Strikland and Jonas Wood and so goes westward so far as Cheacanoe hath marked, being purchased in August last, which was 1658."

The westernmost neck, Half Neck, bordered by Ketchams Creek and Howell Creek, is the modern site of the Amity Harbor neighborhood, including Tanner Park. Great Neck, situated between Howell Creek and Great Neck Creek, is now known as Copiague Harbor. According to William Wallace Tooker, the Native Americans originally referred to Great Neck as "Tatamuckatakis," meaning "meadow that trembles." The eastern of the three necks, Copiague Neck, which lies between Great Neck Creek and Strongs Creek (sometimes referred to as Copiague Creek), became the American Venice neighborhood. Huntington settlers traveling from the northern village through Huntington South to the Great South Bay followed paths through the wooded plains established by the Native Americans. At the head of the necks was a trail that would become South Country Road, now Montauk Highway.

The 1700s brought a local gristmill for grinding grain and a sawmill for cutting lumber along Montauk Highway. During the 19th century, the country settlement of primarily farming families also included a cloth mill and later a paper mill, which were operated using waterpower from the local creeks. Goods made in these mills were shipped to markets by horse and wagon. By the mid-1800s, a stagecoach route brought visitors from New York City, and the first locomotive of the South Side Railroad passed through Copiague in 1867.

In the mid-19th century, the south shore of Huntington town had a number of family farms and three sizeable communities, namely Amityville, Babylon, and Breslau (later Lindenhurst). Despite its growing numbers, the center of Huntington town activity remained in the north, and many residents of Huntington South became dissatisfied with the town. The first printed suggestion of dividing the town of Huntington appeared in the February 12, 1870, edition of the *South Side Signal* newspaper, which began publishing in Babylon village in June 1869. Citing the rapid growth of the south shore communities and control of those southern communities by the northern Huntington village, Henry Livingston, founder and editor of the *Signal*, stated, "Huntington is large enough in territory to make two good-sized towns, while the rapid increase of population on the South Side will allow this half to govern itself. We feel kindly towards the North Side . . . but the Village of Huntington cannot much longer make law for Babylon."

In 1872, Huntington South residents favorably voted to secede from Huntington and formed the town of Babylon. The new town took its name from its largest community and later adopted a town seal incorporating an eagle, representing the national bird, and images of a fish, clam, oyster, and eel, symbolizing the significance of the new town's adjacency to the Great South Bay.

Copiague's position between the two burgeoning villages of Amityville and Lindenhurst led to the growth of the community, but it is likely that its location contributed to its lack of identity as well. The small rural community would often be inaccurately identified as Amityville or Lindenhurst or just "between Amityville and Lindenhurst" until the mid-20th century. Throughout the 19th century, the Copiague area went by several names: "East Amityville" came from its proximity to the adjacent community, references to the community as "Powells" reflects the predominance of the Powell family in the Copiague-Amityville communities, and that name "Great Neck" was well suited, deriving its name from the peninsula along its southern shore, but the name caused confusion with the northern Long Island community of the same name. For reasons still uncertain, the name Copiague was officially adopted in the 1890s. In the early 20th century, the name Marconiville, a neighborhood north of the railroad tracks on either side of Great Neck Road, was synonymous with Copiague. In the 1920s, Marconiville residents petitioned the U.S. Post Office and Long Island Rail Road to change the names of their local stations from Copiague to Marconiville; however, they were unsuccessful.

Today Copiague is one of 10 hamlets in the town of Babylon. Derived from the Middle English term for a small village or rural settlement, the term "hamlet" is used in New York State to denote unincorporated communities within towns. The town of Babylon also includes the hamlets of Deer Park, East Farmingdale, North Amityville, North Babylon, North Lindenhurst, West Babylon, Wheatley Heights, Wyandanch, the barrier beach communities, and the incorporated villages of Amityville, Babylon, and Lindenhurst. According to the 2000 U.S. Census, the town of Babylon is the most densely populated town in Suffolk County with over 211,000 residents. More than 10 percent of the town of Babylon residents live in Copiague, a community small in size—just 3.2 square miles—compared with its great history.

One book could never completely contain the awesome complexity of Copiague's vast history, one that grows with each person who embraces the community as their own. Presented here is a visual narrative of Copiague history designed to continue the tradition of sharing Copiague history and to honor the community's heritage. It builds upon the contributions made by other Copiague authors who established a cherished custom of sharing Copiague history, namely Elizabeth Eide, Walter G. O'Connell, and Angelo Vacca. My hope is for this book to continue that legacy and inspire others to preserve Copiague's history—past, present, and future.

—Mary Cascone, C.A.
Office of Historic Services, Town of Babylon

One

EARLY COPIAGUE

The Copiague community was first settled by English and Dutch settlers from the northern community of Huntington who traveled to the lands along the Great South Bay to gather salt hay used to feed livestock or other domestic purposes. Great Neck Road, shown in this early-20th-century postcard, became the main thoroughfare through the growing community. (AHS.)

GREAT NECK ROAD, Copiague, L. I.

Great Neck Road, as shown here, was lined with large trees and homes. Prior to World War II and the subsequent population explosion of the 1950s, Copiague was a rural community, with many of its residents relying on their own crops and livestock for food. Beginning in the late 1800s, the south shore of Long Island also became a popular summer vacation locale for New York City dwellers. (AHS.)

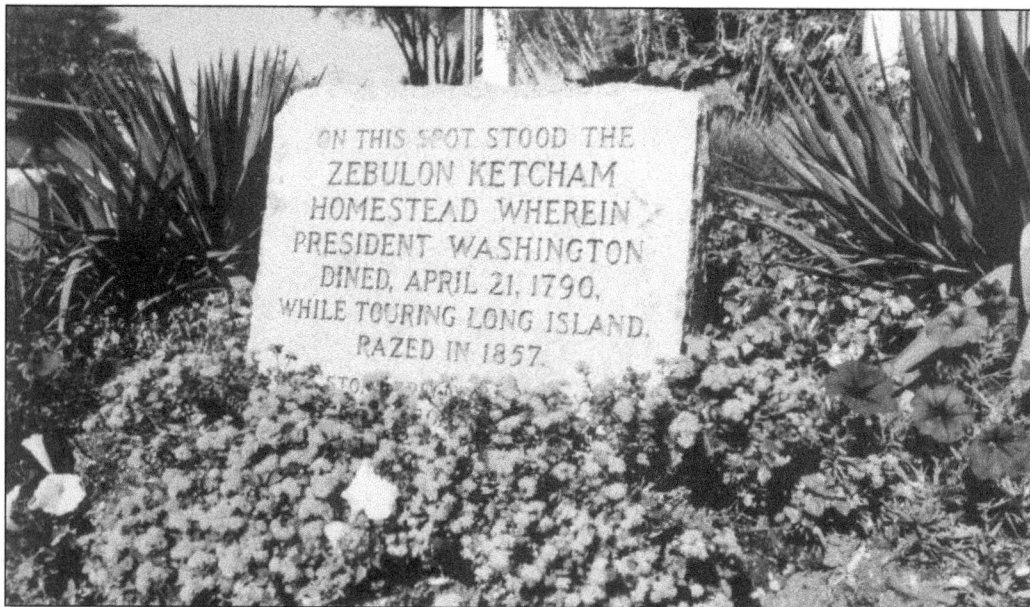

ON THIS SPOT STOOD THE
ZEBULON KETCHAM
HOMESTEAD WHEREIN
PRESIDENT WASHINGTON
DINED, APRIL 21, 1790,
WHILE TOURING LONG ISLAND,
RAZED IN 1857.

Pres. George Washington visited Copiague, then known as "Huntington South," during his tour of Long Island in the spring of 1790. In 1927, the Babylon Town Board erected a memorial stone to commemorate his historic visit, reading, "On this spot stood the Zebulon Ketcham Homestead wherein President Washington dined, April 21, 1790, while touring Long Island. Razed in 1857." However, some believe that Ketcham's home was not destroyed. (Rodi.)

On April 20, 1790, the 58-year-old president crossed the East River and traveled to Jamaica. The next morning, he and his traveling companions began their five-day, 165-mile journey, making stops at Hempstead to water and feed the horse and at the Ketcham homestead for dinner before spending the evening at Sagtikos Manor in West Bay Shore. Zebulon Ketcham had been a member of the local militia during the Revolutionary War.

Traveling in a cream-colored coach led by four gray horses, Washington wrote the following in his diary on April 21, 1790: "We fell into the South Rd. [Montauk Highway] . . . We dined at one Ketcham's [which] had also been a public House [an inn] . . . a very neat and decent one." Having left Jamaica at 8:00 a.m., the president arrived at Ketcham's around 4:00 p.m.

The Ketcham homestead was located near the intersection of Deauville Boulevard and Montauk Highway where the stone marker sits. The home of Zebulon and Hannah Ketcham was an unpainted shingle-style house. Historians note that there were two Ketcham houses that stood side by side. One perished in 1857, while the other, shown here, was relocated to Amityville and is asserted to be the dwelling visited by the president.

Washington and his traveling party shared a meal with the Ketcham family. Some historians report that the president presented a gold ring to one of Ketcham's children, while others have said he presented a coin to the child. The table from Ketcham's Inn, at which the president dined, is part of the collections of the Huntington Historical Society and is on display at the c. 1750 David Conklin Farmhouse Museum.

Jacob Smith, with his delivery wagon in 1898, operated a dairy on the southwest corner of Great Neck Road and Oak Street. Smith's sons, William and Robin, helped with the dairy business and were known to direct 60 cows between the dairy and meadowlands, which later became Amity Harbor, forcing automobiles on Montauk Highway to wait for the passing herd. The dairy later moved to Amityville. (AHS.)

Thomas Powell, 11th supervisor of the Town of Babylon (1896–1899), was the only town supervisor from Copiague. Born on his family's farm on the north side of Montauk Highway, Powell lived and worked on the farm until just a few months before his death. Although he attended school only until the age of 16, the farmer Powell was also a school trustee, bank director, and tax assessor.

15

Seen here is the home and farm of Irving T. Powell, which was located along the south side of Montauk Highway. Members of the extended Powell family resided throughout the Copiague-Amityville area. The fact that the Copiague area was at one time referred to as "Powell's" signifies the family's prevalence in the community. (AHS.)

Although this postcard image lists its address as Amityville, the Savoy Inn was formerly located on the south side of Montauk Highway in Copiague, west of Great Neck Road. Aviators from a flying field across the street frequented the Savoy Inn. It has also been reported that dirigibles landed and took off from that neighboring airfield. (AHS.)

POST OFFICE BLOCK, Copiague, L. I.

By the early 20th century, trolleys were a popular form of transportation. In 1910, the South Shore Traction Company electrified an existing horse-drawn trolley line between the Babylon railroad station and the docks and extended the line westward through West Babylon, Lindenhurst, and Copiague to the Amityville railroad station. The trolley tracks were laid along Oak Street, past the post office shown here. (Cahaney.)

OAK STREET, Copiague, L. I.

Westbound trolleys entered Copiague near Strong and West Gates Avenues, proceeding northwest toward Florida Avenue and Great Neck Road. The trolley line continued north to Oak Street, where it turned west toward Amityville. This westward view shows the trolley tracks along Oak Street. In Amityville, passengers could connect with the northbound Cross-Island trolley, operated by the Huntington Railroad Company from 1909 to 1919, along a course that later became Route 110. (AHS.)

On June 11, 1910, a Babylon to Amityville trolley line opened with five small trolley cars, each carrying 28 passengers. The fare from Copiague was 5¢, while the full trip from Amityville to Babylon cost 10¢ for the 35-minute ride. Stories of trolley mishaps abound. Reportedly, passenger weight needed to be distributed evenly in the cars otherwise they would tip. (VBHPS.)

Henry Ellis Willmont, a former motorman, recalled that the trolley "used to jump off [the track] quite a bit and we'd have to run it back on." This postcard view shows the trolley traveling eastbound on Oak Street. The growing popularity of automobiles and the hardships of World War I led to the demise of trolley ridership and operations of the Babylon Railroad Company ended on May 25, 1920. (AHS.)

The South Side Railroad began operation in 1860. The railroad first passed through the Copiague community in 1867, when the South Side Railroad extended service eastward through Amityville and into the village of Babylon. The South Side Railroad became part of the Long Island Rail Road in 1874, and arrivals at the Copiague station first appeared in 1901 timetables. (Ziel.)

The Long Island Rail Road station at Copiague, located east of Great Neck Road on the south side of Marconi Boulevard, is shown here looking east in this 1930s scene. The first Copiague depot was built around 1900 on property donated by neighboring resident Scudder Jervis. Funds to construct the depot building were raised by local citizens. The need for a depot was a reflection of the community's growth. (Calandrino-Natalie.)

Great Neck Road is seen here looking north from the railroad tracks in April 1949. The small shanty (at left) sheltered the gate man who was responsible for manually raising and lowering the crossing gates before they became automatic. The railroad crossings could be dangerous, and reports of train accidents with automobiles and pedestrians were an unfortunate but common occurrence in many communities along the branch line. (Ziel.)

This is a 21st-century view of the south side of the Copiague station of the Long Island Rail Road. The grade-level station house stood until 1967, when the railroad tracks along the Babylon branch were elevated. On average, more than 50 trains deliver passengers to and from the Copiague train station every day. (Rodi.)

Two

NATIVE AMERICAN HERITAGE

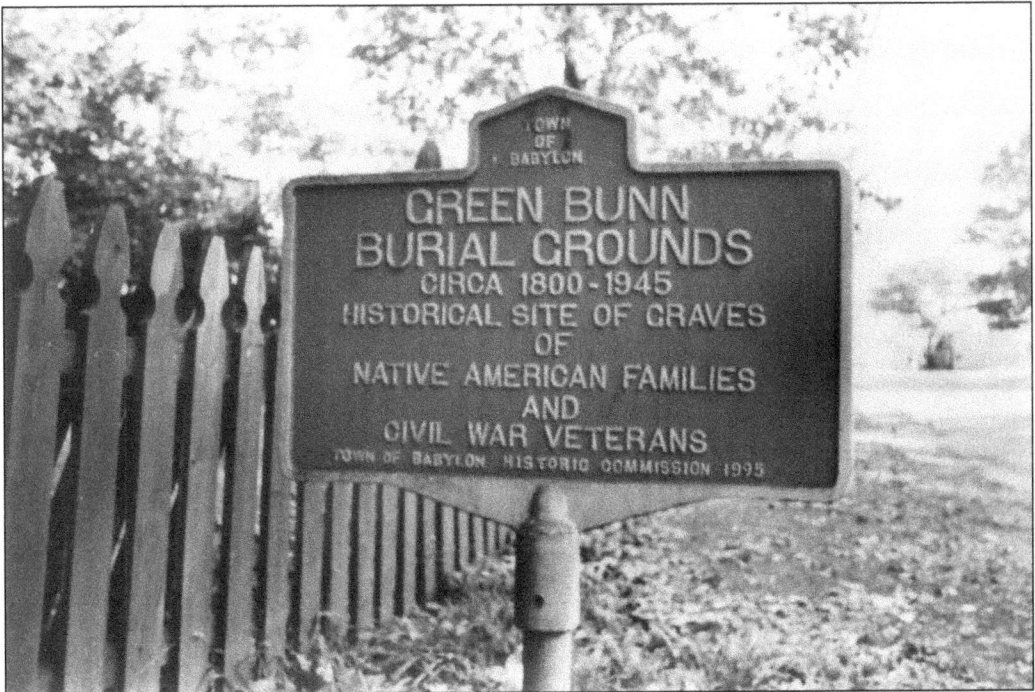

The Green-Bunn and Brewster Burial Grounds were the final resting places for many Native American families and Civil War veterans. In 1995, historical markers were placed at the cemetery entrances by the Town of Babylon Historic Preservation Commission. The unassuming burial grounds flank both sides of Bethpage Road, north of Sunrise Highway near the border of Copiague and North Amityville. (Rodi.)

In 1994, the Babylon Town Board officially designated the Green-Bunn and Brewster Burial Grounds as local historic landmarks. The following year, community residents, with the help of the Town of Babylon, rededicated the historical burial grounds with the placing of historical markers and the erection of two newly designed monuments.

The Green-Bunn Burial Grounds monument rests on a stone in the shape of a tortoise and was designed with the stones resting upon one another as an artistic expression of a family or community group. The reptile-inspired monument is inscribed with the family names of Byard, Chepo (Chiphouse), Edmonds, Green, Payne, and Wopwasbunn (Bunn), paying homage to the ancestors of these families who rest in this hallowed ground. (Rodi.)

Similar in design to the Green-Bunn monument, the Brewster Burial Grounds memorial is dedicated "In Memory of the First Native American Families of Long Island and Those Known Only to the Great Spirit." The family names of Carr, Douglas, Hubbs-Hicks, Steele, Valentine, and Yamaqua (Brewster) are inscribed thereon. The graves of both burial grounds date back to around 1800. (Rodi.)

Resting in the shade of towering trees along the west side of Bethpage Road, these three concrete statues have captured the interest and imaginations of local residents for decades. These statues are everlasting memorials to Florance H. Brewster, Sidney Brewster, and Charlie Carr, a veteran of the Civil War. (Rodi.)

This memorial to Florance H. Brewster was carved from cement blocks in the early 1950s by her nephew, Richard Brewster, a cement mason. The statue was once painted with a reddish face and black hair, together with glass marble eyes. While much of the tinted elements have faded, the statue figure still holds fast to the axe carved in her hands. Sidney Brewster was the father of Richard Brewster. (Rodi.)

This sculpture was designed and inscribed by Richard Brewster to honor "Charlie Carr, Civil War Veteran." A 1955 newspaper reporter described the figure as having "Indian features . . . a brown painted face and black painted hair." Richard Brewster was quoted as proudly saying, "Some of my people fought for Gen. Washington, and others were soldiers in the Civil War and the Spanish-American War, as well as all other wars." (Rodi.)

Three

MARCONIVILLE

The alluring history of Copiague's Marconiville community begins with the acquaintance of two men: Giovanni "John" Campagnoli and Guglielmo Marconi, the world famous inventor of wireless technology. The two men met while attending Italy's University of Bologna. Marconi inscribed this photograph to Campagnoli as Fondatore di Marconiville, "the founder of Marconiville," in 1920. (LePorte.)

Guglielmo Marconi received his first patent for wireless telegraphy in 1896 and five years later made the first wireless transmission across the Atlantic Ocean. Marconi shared the 1909 Nobel Prize in physics with Karl Ferdinand Braun. In later years, it was determined that Marconi could not lay exclusive claim to all of his reported wireless discoveries; however, during his lifetime, Marconi was remarkably celebrated around the world. (VBHPS.)

Giovanni "John" Campagnoli was an Italian engineer who reportedly made his fortune in the bicycle business. Around 1906, the Sovereign Realty Company of New York City purchased the Brinckerhoff Manor property north of the railroad, which would later become Marconiville. Campagnoli became vice president of Sovereign Realty in 1908. Assuming the presidency of the company the following year, Campagnoli moved his family to Copiague and orchestrated the community's progress. (LePorte.)

On May 17, 1915, using stationery from the Marconi Wireless Telegraph Company of America, Guglielmo Marconi wrote to John Campagnoli thanking him for his letter and cards of Marconiville, "which I was very pleased to have . . . it would give me much pleasure to visit that village and I hope soon to be able to inform you when I will be able to do so." (LePorte.)

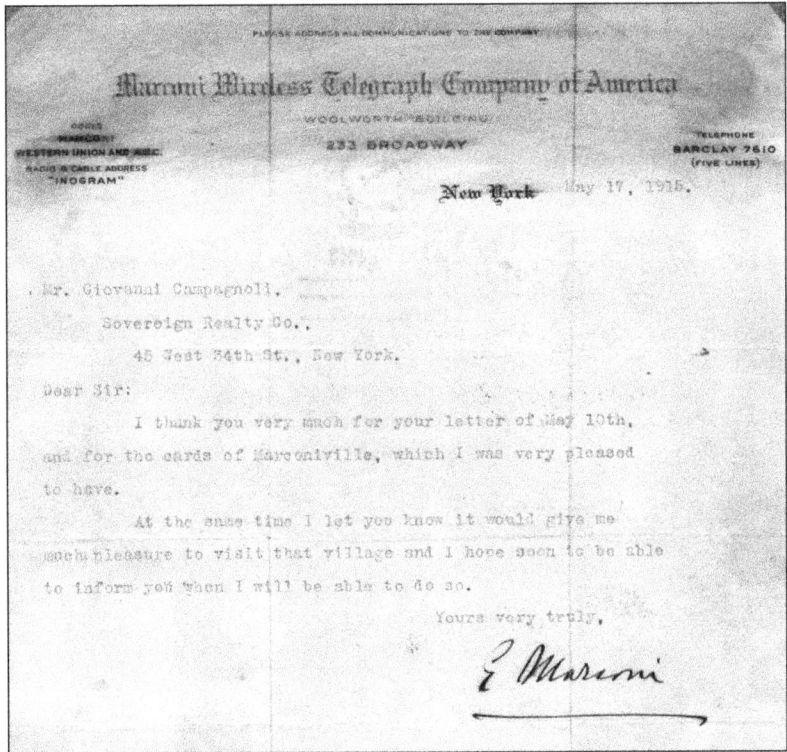

Pictured here is an envelope used for a wireless message transmitted by the Marconi Wireless Telegraph Company of Canada Limited, known as a "Marconigram." Revolutionary technology at that time, early-20th-century ships were equipped with Marconi Rooms in which trained Marconi operators were responsible for transmitting wireless Marconigrams to and from other ships and land. The Marconi operators aboard the RMS *Titanic* are credited with transmitting distress signals that aided rescue efforts. (LePorte.)

This eye-catching three-story home was the residence of John Campagnoli. Reportedly, the Great Neck Road house was adorned with marble statues and two ceramic plaques depicting a Native American man and woman. Campagnoli remained a prominent presence in the community until 1948, when he and his wife returned to Italy. He passed away two years later at the age of 85. (VBHPS.)

The parklike grounds of John Campagnoli's home were adorned with marbled driveways, manicured trees, and decorative planters. In the background of this jovial c. 1950 photograph the ornate benches and fountains set in the exterior garden wall can be seen. The Campagnoli home, later donated to Our Lady of the Assumption Church, remained a community icon for many years before succumbing to the ravages of time. (LePorte.)

The famous inventor Guglielmo Marconi (center) made two known visits to Copiague's Marconiville in 1917 and 1927. John Campagnoli (left) was an integral part of the Marconiville-Copiague community. Copiague residents have recalled childhood memories of Campagnoli as a somewhat mysterious figure who was known for donning a dramatic-looking black cape and large hat. (LePorte.)

John Campagnoli and his guests greet Guglielmo Marconi in 1917. Like the neighborhood's name itself, most Marconiville street names were chosen in honor of famous Italian scientists, explorers, artists, and locales: Amerigo Vespucci, Alessandro Volta, Leonardo DaVinci, Prince Ludovico Chigi della Rovere Albani, Pope Pius XI, Corsica, Malta, Imola, and Sicily. (VBHPS.)

John Campagnoli, standing behind Guglielmo Marconi who is wearing a hat (above), made many lasting contributions to the Copiague-Marconiville community, including the donation of land for the construction of Our Lady of the Assumption Catholic Church on Molloy Street and the World War I Veterans Memorial, now situated in Veterans Memorial Park at the southeast corner of Marconi Boulevard and Great Neck Road. (VBHPS.)

The Marconiville area has been home to immigrants from around the world, beginning with Colonial Dutch settlers and Italian, Polish, and Hispanic immigrants who made Copiague their home. Guglielmo Marconi himself was a citizen of the world. The son of an Italian country gentleman and an Irish mother, Marconi spent his childhood education between both of his parents' native countries. (VBHPS.)

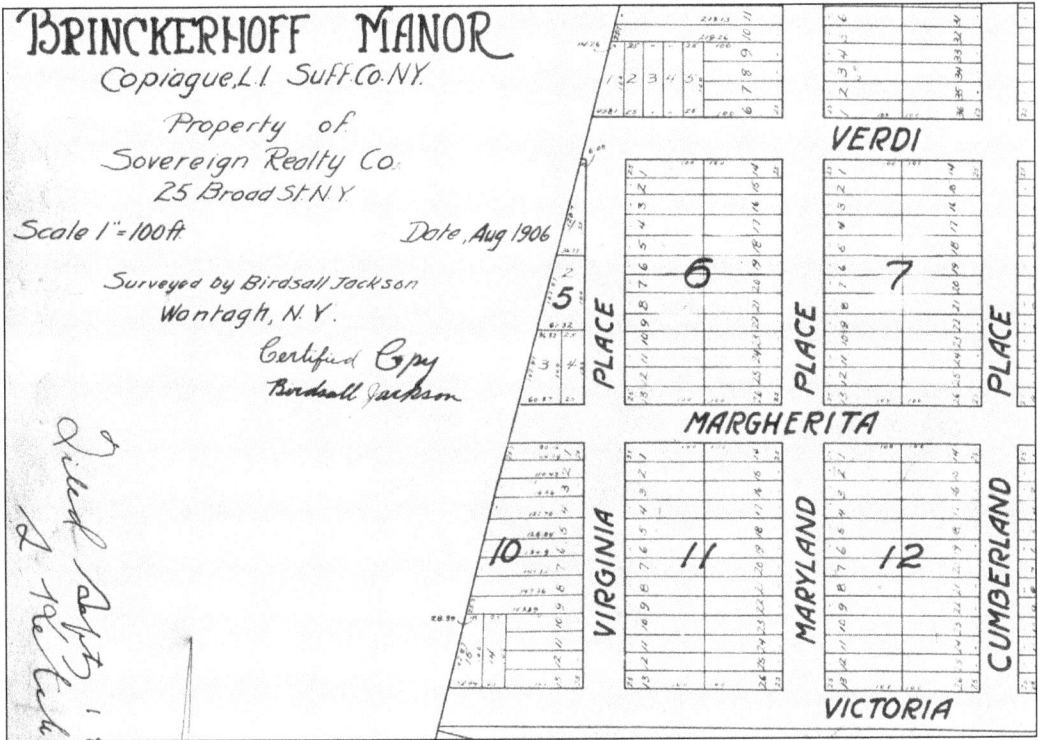

BRINCKERHOFF MANOR

Copiague, L.I. Suff. Co. N.Y.

Property of
Sovereign Realty Co.
25 Broad St. N.Y.

Scale 1"=100 ft   Date, Aug 1906

Surveyed by Birdsall Jackson
Wantagh, N.Y.

Certified Copy
Birdsall Jackson

VERDI

6   7

PLACE   PLACE   PLACE

MARGHERITA

10   11   12

VIRGINIA   MARYLAND   CUMBERLAND

VICTORIA

Prior to Sovereign Realty Company's purchase of the property, the area was known as Brinkerhoff Manor. The Brinkerhoffs were one of many Dutch families that emigrated from the Netherlands to colonial Long Island in the 18th century. Eventually one branch of the family settled in Huntington South, the present-day town of Babylon, and made Copiague their home.

Following World War II, there were some who challenged the propriety of the community's Italian street names and petitioned for their conversion. Such sentiments may explain the apparent change of a few street names; however, the majority of the names remain as a lasting memory of Campagnoli's desire to accentuate the accomplishments of pioneering Italians such as Guglielmo Marconi, seen here enjoying his visit to his namesake community. (LePorte.)

Arriving at the Marconi Hotel on Sunday, July 17, 1917, Guglielmo Marconi (third from left) and his companions were greeted by dozens of Marconiville residents. The following week, the *Amityville Record* reported that Marconi was "entertained at the home of John Campagnoli. After dinner he made a little speech to a crowd gathered in the village and stood for a number of photographs." (VBHPS.)

During his visit, Marconi was presented with flowers from Henrietta Bernagozzi (center, wearing a sash). According to Angelo Vacca, author of *Intimate Portraits of Old Copiague*, she remarked, in Italian, "I bring greetings from all the residents of Marconiville, who are overjoyed and honored. I offer you this simple flower, with devotion and respect to you and an ever wonderful Italy. Long live Marconi—long live Italy." (LePorte.)

One of the most famous amenities of the Italian American enclave was the Marconi Hotel, or Marconiville Hotel, which stood on the north side of Marconi Boulevard near the present-day Copiague Post Office. Built around 1910, the community landmark, a three-story cement-block structure, succumbed to a devastating fire on June 8, 1925. (LePorte.)

Attracting city-weary lodgers to the rural Copiague community along the Great South Bay, the following advertisement appeared in the *New York Times* on May 29, 1919: "Marconi Inn, Copiague, L.I., with all improvements; large airy rooms; excellent cuisine; bathing, boating, fishing five minutes away; is an ideal place for the Summer; moderate rates, Frank DiBugno, Manager." (Gusmano.)

Finest fishing
and sailing on
the Atlantic Coast.

Supplies for sailing
parties furnished
on short notice.

MARCONI HOTEL, MARCONIVILLE, L. I.

Another landmark lost was the display of large concrete letters spelling "Marconiville," which stood alongside the railroad tracks. Passengers arriving by train were met with the welcoming display. The name "Marconiville" also appeared in the railroad time schedules. The railroad's endorsement of the Marconiville name caused confusion for some passengers, unaware that the Marconiville station was also the Copiague station. Reportedly, the concrete letters were removed in the 1940s. (Cahaney.)

One of the many Italian families that made Marconiville their American home was the Bernagozzi family. In his hometown of Cesena, Italy, near Bologna, Robert Bernagozzi became acquainted with John Campagnoli, who owned a bicycle company in Italy. Bernagozzi's brother William was the first to purchase a home in Marconiville and was soon followed by his siblings Robert, Ferdinand, and Elvira. (LePorte.)

Robert Bernagozzi's family, from left to right, son Cesare, Robert, wife Bruna, son Louis, and daughter Louise pose in front of their Colombo Avenue home near Dixon Avenue around 1924. Bernagozzi owned and operated a food import business in New York City and from his Marconiville home. Bernagozzi was known to import truckloads of grapes from California to his Marconiville home where he distilled his own wine. (LePorte.)

Though it stands a few blocks south of the neighborhood's border, a decorative arch proclaiming "Marconiville" stands near the northwest corner of Hollywood Avenue and Great Neck Road. Reportedly, the arch does not date back to Marconiville's heyday, but rather was erected by a nostalgic community member around the 1980s. (Rodi.)

The Marconiville community is not the only association the town of Babylon has with Guglielmo Marconi. From 1902 until 1907, the Marconi Wireless Telegraph Company operated a wireless transmission station and training facility for wireless operators on Fire Island Avenue in Babylon village, a few miles east of Copiague. The small station, referred to as the "Marconi Shack," is seen at the base of the towering 160-foot transmission pole. (VBHPS.)

The 12-foot-by-12-foot transmission station stood in Babylon village until 1930 when Edwin Howard Armstrong, inventor of FM radio and a great admirer of Marconi, purchased and presented it to the Radio Corporation of America (RCA) in Rocky Point. The Marconi Shack was displayed by RCA for several decades and was later transferred to the grounds of Rocky Point's Frank J. Carasiti Elementary School. (VBHPS.)

Four

AMERICAN VENICE

A residential community designed to emulate the magnificent "City of Canals," Venice, Italy, American Venice was Copiague's premier summer colony along the Great South Bay in the 1920s. The American Venice Corporation declared, "Once you come to know American Venice, once you discover all that lies there, the fires of your imagination will be rekindled, your hopes renewed, your search of an ideal home rewarded."

On September 16, 1925, the newly formed American Venice Corporation purchased the majority of the Copiague Neck, over 360 acres, from the Copiag [sic] Land Company. Construction of the new development quickly ensued. The administration plaza and many of the streets were ready for the Grand Opening on May 23, 1926, though it appears that the only homes constructed at that time were along Alhambra Avenue West (at right). The administration plaza along Montauk Highway was a center of activity for the new community, with people gathering around the newly constructed Grand Canal stretching down to the Great South Bay. By this time, the Santa Barbara Canal, intersecting halfway down the Grand Canal, and the Canal Lugano (upper left) were also completed. The gazebo in the Laguna San Marco is highlighted against the glistening Grand Canal. (Calandrino-Natalie.)

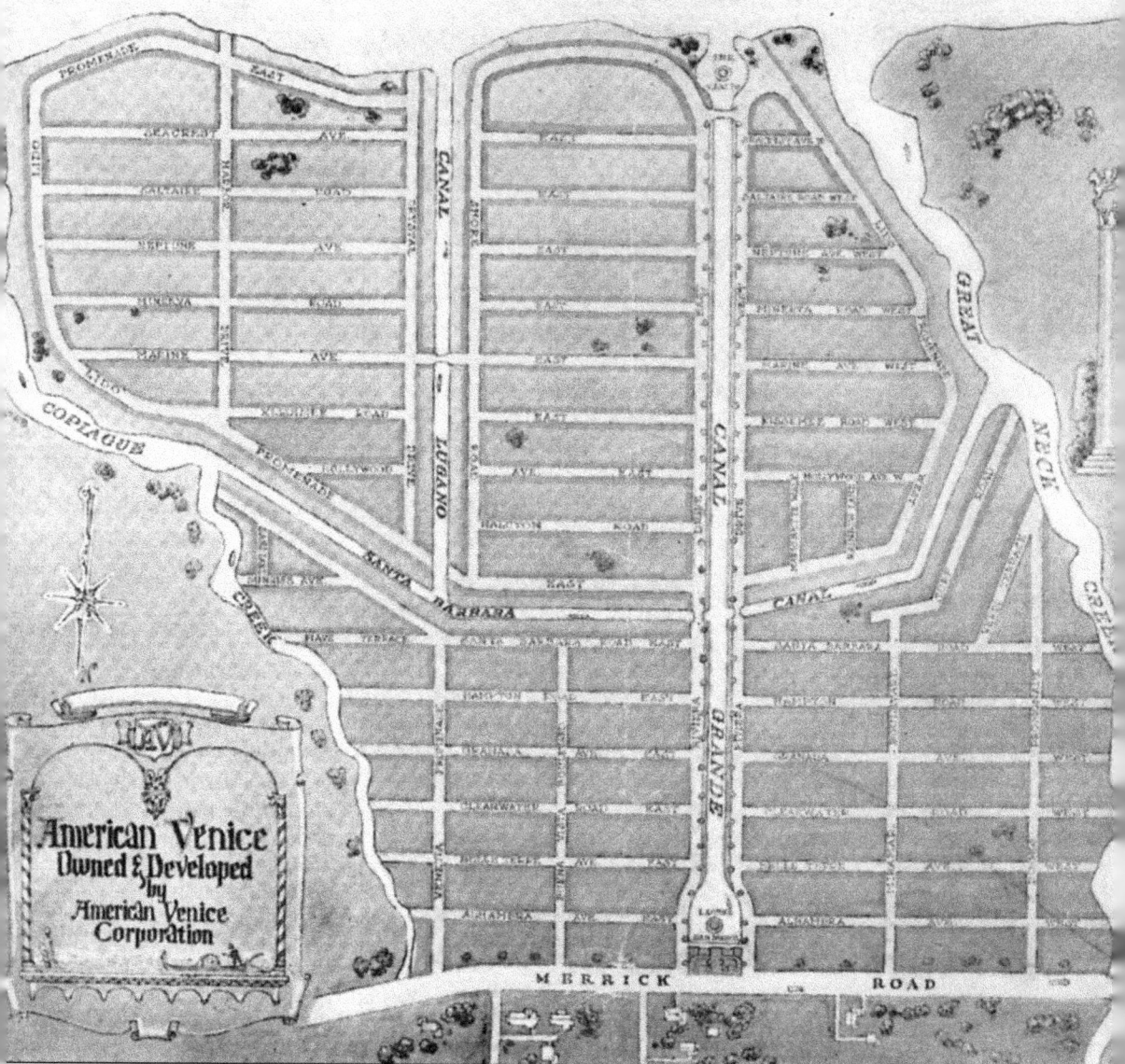

This map of American Venice reveals the original layout of the community about 1926. American Venice was formed from a natural peninsula known as Copiague Neck, bordered by Great Neck Creek on the west, Montauk Highway on the north, Copiague (Strongs) Creek on the east, and the Great South Bay on the south. Three man-made canals—Grand Canal, Santa Barbara Canal, and Canal Lugano—divided the community into five parts.

Prior to American Venice, the Copiague Neck area was an uninhabited marshland, but all that changed in the fall 1925. Attesting to the popularity of the new development, just two months after construction commenced, a local newspaper declared that American Venice had become a "Mecca" for home buyers and that 12 real estate salesmen had assisted customers on a busy Sunday despite heavy rains. (Pisani.)

The first houses built in American Venice appear to have been these five on Alhambra Avenue West—two-story houses with tile roofs and arches in the architecture. Larger than most of the others houses built for new residents, these houses were most likely model homes shown to prospective buyers. (Steinbrecher.)

On October 2, 1925, the local *Amityville Record* proclaimed, "Big Project is Little Venice, Started This Week." The newspaper announced that dredgers would create a 240-foot lagoon from Montauk Highway to the Great South Bay. The *Record* further reported that work had begun with a "steam dredger taking off the top soil. Concrete highways will be started at once." (Steinbrecher.)

The American Venice Corporation advertised their new development in New York City newspapers. Tantalizing images of gondolas rounding striped poles in the canal, fashionable men and women strolling the promenades and bathing beaches, and romantic Italianate cottages lured city dwellers to shed the hassle of urban life and enjoy the pleasures of the bay-front retreat. (Steinbrecher.)

To complete the Venetian fantasy, gondolas were imported from Italy. Advertisements lured prospective real estate buyers from New York City with free transportation and an offer to "come— enjoy a trip on our Gala Gondolas (operated by gondoliers in native costume)." Gondola rides around the community were available to local residents until the mid-1930s. (Steinbrecher.)

A 1926 advertisement announced, "Your Future Home is at American Venice—Here you have the counterpart of old Venice, 'Queen of the Adriatic,' in a modernized setting formerly enjoyed only by the rich. A beauty spot where you can build your own little Venetian Villa at moderate cost and health-giving surroundings. A million miles from dull care, yet only an hour's ride from the heart of New York City." (Pisani.)

The American Venice   Lindenhurst, Long Island, N. Y.

Postcard images of the waterfront development, such as this one depicting a view of the manicured Italian gardens of the administration plaza, typically read, "The American Venice, Lindenhurst, Long Island, N.Y." Situated just west of the Lindenhurst village border, south of Montauk Highway, the American Venice community uses a Lindenhurst mailing address. This dual identity sometimes creates confusion, but American Venice has always been part of Copiague. (LHS.)

The American Venice   Lindenhurst, Long Island, N. Y.

This photograph shows another "Lindenhurst" postcard of American Venice with a view of the ornate gazebo in the Laguna San Marco at the northern end of the Grand Canal. San Marco, or St. Mark, is the patron saint of Venice. Many features and places in American Venice take their names and designs from historic Venice, Italy. (LHS.)

The principals of the dynamic American Venice Corporation were Isaac Meister and Victor Pisani, shown here near his Brooklyn home in the 1920s. Pisani, an Italian native, and Meister developed many hotels and other real estate projects in and around New York City, New Jersey, and Long Island. The 1929 stock market crash took a toll on the real estate corporation, which declared bankruptcy in July 1930. (Pisani.)

As an infant, Lorraine Valerio Prisco posed with her mother, Jean Valerio, at one of the decorative planters in the administration plaza in 1938. The young Lorraine enjoyed summers in American Venice at her grandfather's bungalow on Kissimee Road East. The real estate sales office for the development is seen in the background. (Prisco.)

Like many city dwellers, the Mazzoli family moved to American Venice in the 1930s to enjoy its peaceful south shore and country atmosphere. Shown here, Lottie Mazzoli strikes a playful pose against the charming backdrop of the American Venice plaza. On the left side of this photograph are the steps that led down to the Laguna San Marco where one could embark on a gondola ride around the community. (Mazzoli.)

The winged-lion is the symbol of St. Mark, patron saint of Venice. The winged-lion columns on the American Venice plaza are replicas of the one in the Piazza San Marco (St. Mark's Square), Venice, Italy. Although winged-lions abound throughout Venice, there is only one winged-lion column in the Piazza San Marco. American Venice was bestowed with two majestic beasts that stand guard from their lofty perches. (Mazzoli.)

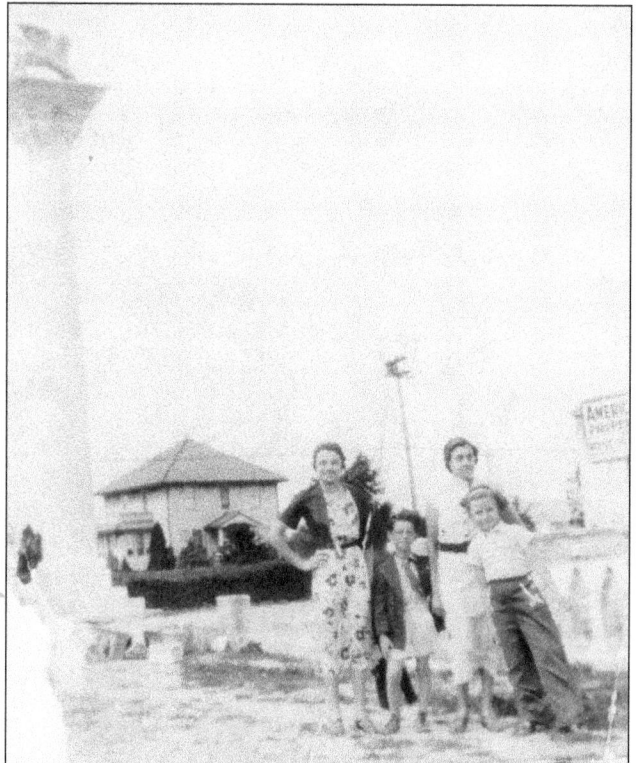

Along with the Venetian bridges, the towering winged-lion columns are the most recognizable features of the old American Venice. For older community residents, even today, their image can illicit the memories of strolling along the plaza grounds surrounding the Laguna San Marco, as depicted in these images recorded by the Mazzoli family. (Mazzoli.)

Features of the old American Venice plaza have since been hidden from view; however, the two columns topped with winged-lions still stand along Montauk Highway. Though they have sometimes been referred to as griffins, winged-lions—having the body of a lion with the wings of a majestic bird—are not griffins. The two mythical beasts have similarities, but a griffin possesses the head of a bird. (Rodi.)

Members of the Valerio-Filippone family strike a relaxed summertime pose in 1938. Developers proclaimed American Venice "The Homeland Charmingly Different" with "the charming homes, the lovely canals . . . the sparkling jewel of the Great Lagoon, the rustic Old World bridges, the gliding gondolas. And, ever present, the waters of the Great South Bay lapping lazily all the day upon a beach." (Prisco.)

This view of the south side of the administration plaza was taken from the Laguna San Marco in 1938. The administration plaza was the community gateway, and the twin buildings housed the sales offices of the American Venice Corporation. Steps from the plaza led down to the dock for gondola rides. (Prisco.)

48

The arrival of gondolas at American Venice was cause for celebration, according to the *Amityville Record* on April 16, 1926: "Gondolas at Venice—Four of the fleet of 20 gondolas which have been ordered for the American Venice development in Lindenhurst arrived from Italy, where they were built, on the S.S. 'Lucia' Saturday." (LHS.)

Striped poles lining the perimeter of the Laguna San Marco replicated the mooring poles used in the canals of Venice, Italy. Inviting prospective buyers to personally tour the new community, the American Venice Corporate avowed, "Any written attempt to portray the charm, the values, the magnitude of the task accomplished at American Venice is sadly inadequate." (Steinbrecher.)

A romantic vision of the gazebo is reflected in the gentle waters of the Laguna San Marco. Grand opening flyers decreed, "A turquoise lagoon under aquamarine sky! Lazy gondolas! Beautiful Italian Gardens! Is it Venice on the Adriatic? No—Venice in America!" Bands were often brought to play from the gazebo centered in the Laguna San Marco, including Long Island's own Guy Lombardo. (Steinbrecher.)

In *A Backward Glance*, Elodie Dibbins wrote of the lagoon, "Soft music drifted across the water from the streamer bedecked bandstand located in the center of a large lagoon. Imported gondolas waited to transport adventurous visitors down broad canals and under picturesque bridges; while those less daring picnicked on the grass, strolled in the Italian gardens, or enjoyed the view from a broad veranda facing the Grand Canal." (Steinbrecher.)

A canopied gondola-style boat rounds the sister gazebo at the south end of the Grand Canal where it joins the Great South Bay. The southern gazebo island was named the Rialto, after the oldest and most famous of the three bridges that span Venice's Grand Canal—the Rialto Bridge, or Ponte di Rialto. (Steinbrecher.)

Two Venetian-style bridges were built along the East and West Riviera Drives around 1926. The bridges and the winged-lion columns were reportedly constructed by master plasterer Donald McPherson. In the late 1980s, there was some concern that the bridges along East and West Rivera Drives were no longer suitable for vehicular traffic, and a proposal was made to replace them with flat-steel bridges. (Steinbrecher.)

The American Venice Civic Association, supported by other citizens and community groups, fought to save the bridges, and they were successfully restored by the Town of Babylon in 1989. The bridges remain cherished features of American Venice. Early construction plans called for up to three additional bridges, though only two came to fruition. (Steinbrecher.)

No houses were ever built on the southeast island of American Venice, which was formed by the Santa Barbara and Lugano Canals. In 1964, Babylon town supervisor William T. Lauder negotiated the establishment of the property as a Suffolk County bird sanctuary named Indian Island. There was once a wooden footbridge to the island, as depicted in this sketch by Ron St. Angelo. (CW.)

In 1926, eleven-year-old Louis Steinbrecher's parents purchased four lots on Kissimee Road East. Residents of Astoria, Queens, they purchased the property as a summer residence. Steinbrecher, pictured with his father and brother on one of the Venetian bridges, recalled that his family visited the property often and enjoyed the beaches along the Great South Bay. Before building a home, the Steinbrechers camped on the property in the early years. (Steinbrecher.)

In the 1930s, the Steinbrechers built the first structure on their American Venice parcel—a two-story garage. The tidy building with curtains hanging from the garage door windows acted as the family's summer retreat for several years. After returning from his service in World War II, Louis Steinbrecher purchased the property from his parents and built a year-round home for his new bride, Marie, just east of the garage. (Steinbrecher.)

This 1930s view of the Steinbrechers garage-turned-bungalow depicts the sandy landscape of American Venice. Marie Steinbrecher recalled her mother-in-law's enjoyment of growing all types of plants on the property, a veritable jungle in contrast to city life. No longer an isolated structure, the garage still stands, although slightly modified. (Steinbrecher.)

54

In his 90s, Louis Steinbrecher recalled his early days in American Venice with obvious delight. He shared priceless memories of gondola rides, construction of the Riviera Drive bridges, and details of the administration plaza. From their Kissimee Road East plot, the Steinbrechers could see all the way to the Great South Bay. Here the rare sighting of a blimp is seen above the vast beach community. (Steinbrecher.)

This Venetian Promenade cottage was purchased by Gasper and Elvira Mascari in the 1930s. An advertisement for this cottage style declared, "$250 Cash Gives You Immediate Possession of This Beautiful Venetian Home—Balance $65 per Month." Early reports stated that the theme for the entire development would be Italian and that no building would be permitted "unless it is more than a faint suggestion of Italian architecture." (Mascari.)

"This faithfully reproduced illustration of a typical Italian Villa at American Venice will open your mind to an entirely new idea of home beauty and artistry," proclaimed a 1927 real estate brochure. "Only a few years ago such a home would have been deemed entirely out of the question for any person in moderate circumstances. Today, fifty of these homes, each distinctly individual, awaits your inspection."

This early cottage on Venetian Promenade, owned by Edward and Lena Liguori, is similar to the artist's rendering shown above. The Liguori's nephew, Hugo Mascari, is pictured at the front gate. In 1927, this cottage style offered "five rooms and bath, each beautifully planned; a modern kitchen and equipped laundry; a spacious sun parlor; a wide veranda and a cellar" for just $6,750. (Mascari.)

This charming stucco cottage was built in the late 1920s along Belle Terre Avenue East, where it remains today. Dotted among the more than 1,000 homes in 21st-century American Venice, a handful of cottages can still be found with original American Venice details, including stucco exteriors, arched doorways and windows, and tiled roofs.

After the American Venice Corporation declared bankruptcy in 1930, an array of different companies built cottages throughout the community. This airy bungalow, located on Kissimee Avenue East, was purchased by Louis Filippone in the early 1930s and exemplifies one of the many new home styles. (Prisco.)

In the years following the untimely demise of the American Venice Corporation, Venetian-style cottages gave way to a variety of summer bungalow styles, including this one that resembled a frontier log cabin. Lottie and Peter Mazzoli pose in front of their Surf Road cottage around 1932. Their home was the builder's model for that bucolic home style. (Mazzoli.)

The Mazzolis moved to American Venice from Brooklyn in the early 1930s. By the end of that decade, they renovated their log cabin–style bungalow to this Colonial design. Blueprints for this quaint five-room home describe it as a "Model Colonial Bungalow," fitted with a kitchen, living room, two bedrooms, and a bath. (Mazzoli.)

Swimming in the canals and easy access to the Great South Bay were key attractions for many American Venice homeowners. As the American Venice Corporation advertised, "There is the unexcelled bathing and swimming in the sparkling waters of the Great South Bay—crystal clear and undefiled." (Mazzoli.)

Cousins Clara and Pat Mazzoli stroll along Miramar Boulevard in the 1930s. The dirt road and scrub oak plains of this vintage summer scene are a stark contrast to the modern community. The growth of American Venice was slow from the mid-1920s through the 1940s, but that changed after World War II. Like much of Long Island, American Venice faced an upsurge of new residents from the suburban expansion of the 1950s. (Mazzoli.)

Five

SUBURBAN EXPANSION

The decade following World War I brought increased home ownership across the country, and Long Island was no exception. Numerous housing developments sprang up along the south shore in the mid-1920s. One noteworthy development was named Amity Harbor, depicting its proximity to the Great South Bay and the village of Amityville. Amity Harbor was the endeavor of Russian immigrant George J. Brown, who flourished in New York City real estate.

Early advertising described the bay-front community as "exclusive, but not expensive . . . created and maintained for nice people. The houses are well built and contain seven rooms of good size, fully equipped with modern improvements. You can keep your car in your own garage and your boat in back of your house." George Brown was a recognizable fixture in the community's early years, often seen riding around in his Packard automobile. Located at the north end of the community's central canal along George Brown Plaza, the yacht club (right) was designed as a community gathering place and had a myriad of occupants before becoming a restaurant in the 1950s. The 55-foot lighthouse (left) offered visitors a view of the Great South Bay. The observation tower was a community landmark for decades, until it was destroyed by Hurricane Gloria in 1985. (AHS.)

The yacht club was forfeited by the 1930s. Michael's Pier III Restaurant was the final resident of the former yacht club before closing its doors in 1992. The building was razed in 1997 and replaced by new homes. George Brown purchased the undeveloped Amity Harbor property from Jerry Johnson; it had previously been used for corn and potato crops, a cow pasture, and hunting grounds. (Rodi.)

Formed in 1934, the Amity Harbor Civic Association is the oldest continuously active civic association in New York State. The Amity Harbor Civic Association maintains a community clubhouse on Western Concourse. Amity Harbor is situated on Copiague's westernmost neck, known as Half Neck. Jonas Wood's 1657 purchase of the property from Chief Wyandance and Keetoseethok referred to it as a "Half Neck of Meadow." (Rodi.)

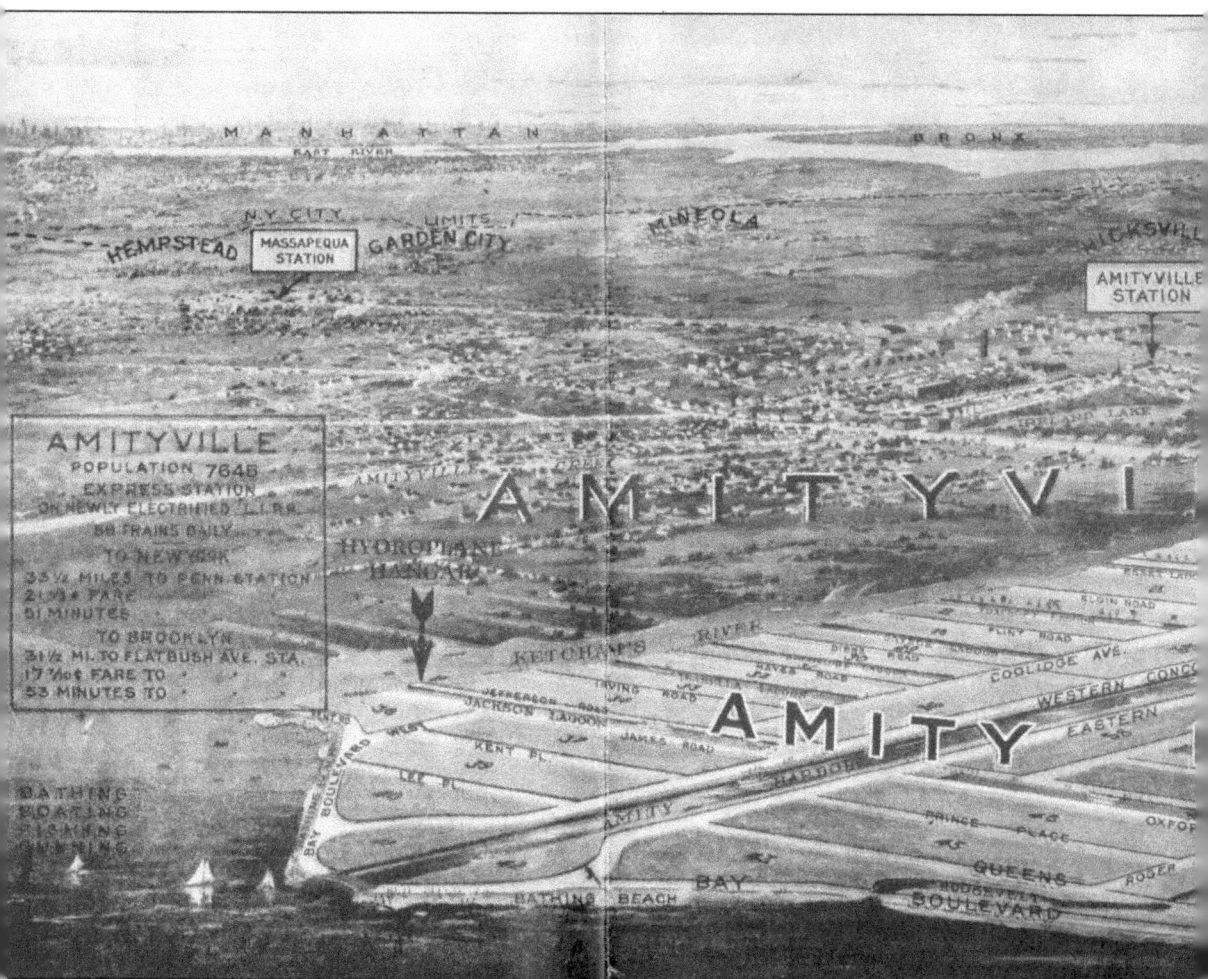

Described as a "sportsman's paradise," Long Island was a recreational playground, offering fishing, hunting, boating, and bathing. Access to boating and boat storage were prominent features in promotions of Amity Harbor, billing the community as "a home for the white-collar man with a car in the front and a boat in the rear." This map of Amity Harbor offers a look at the community's amenities in the mid-1920s: "duck and snipe shooting," "electrified trains," "Sunrise Highway paved

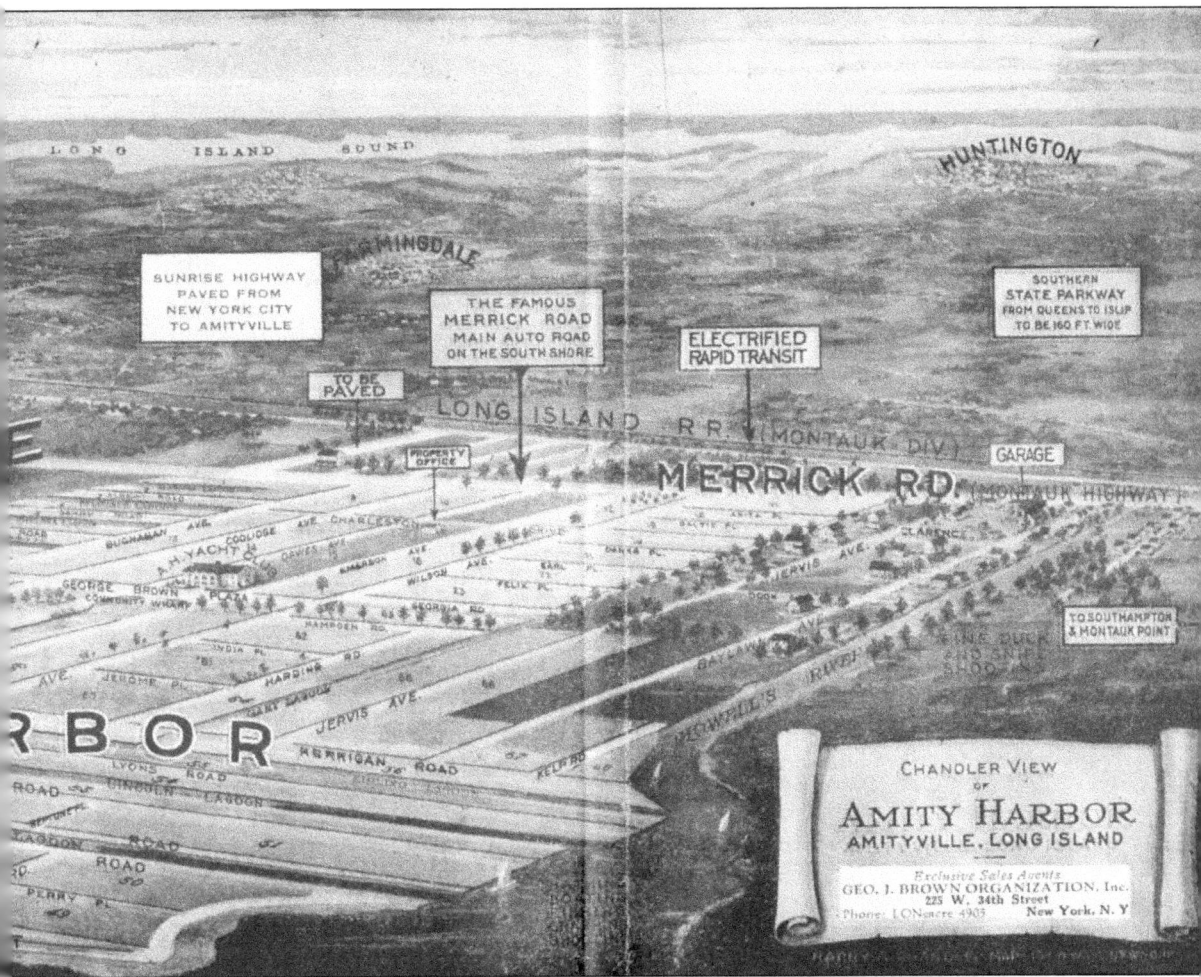

LONG ISLAND SOUND

HUNTINGTON

FARMINGDALE

SUNRISE HIGHWAY
PAVED FROM
NEW YORK CITY
TO AMITYVILLE

THE FAMOUS
MERRICK ROAD
MAIN AUTO ROAD
ON THE SOUTH SHORE

ELECTRIFIED
RAPID TRANSIT

SOUTHERN
STATE PARKWAY
FROM QUEENS TO IS UP
TO BE 160 FT. WIDE

TO BE
PAVED

PROPERTY
OFFICE

LONG ISLAND R. R. (MONTAUK DIV.)

GARAGE

MERRICK RD. (MONTAUK HIGHWAY)

TO SOUTHAMPTON
& MONTAUK POINT

GEORGE BROWN
COMMUNITY WHARF

A M. YACHT CL.

HARBOR

CHANDLER VIEW
OF
AMITY HARBOR
AMITYVILLE, LONG ISLAND

Exclusive Sales Agents
GEO. J. BROWN ORGANIZATION, Inc.
225 W. 34th Street
Phone: LONacre 4903   New York, N. Y.

to Amityville." The Long Island Rail Road electrified the lines through Copiague-Amityville on May 21, 1925. Before 1931–1932, Sunrise Highway was paved only as far east as Amityville. During the Depression, George Brown reportedly relinquished a 93-acre parcel in the southeastern part of the development to satisfy unpaid taxes. The tract was later transferred to the Town of Babylon and developed as Tanner Park.

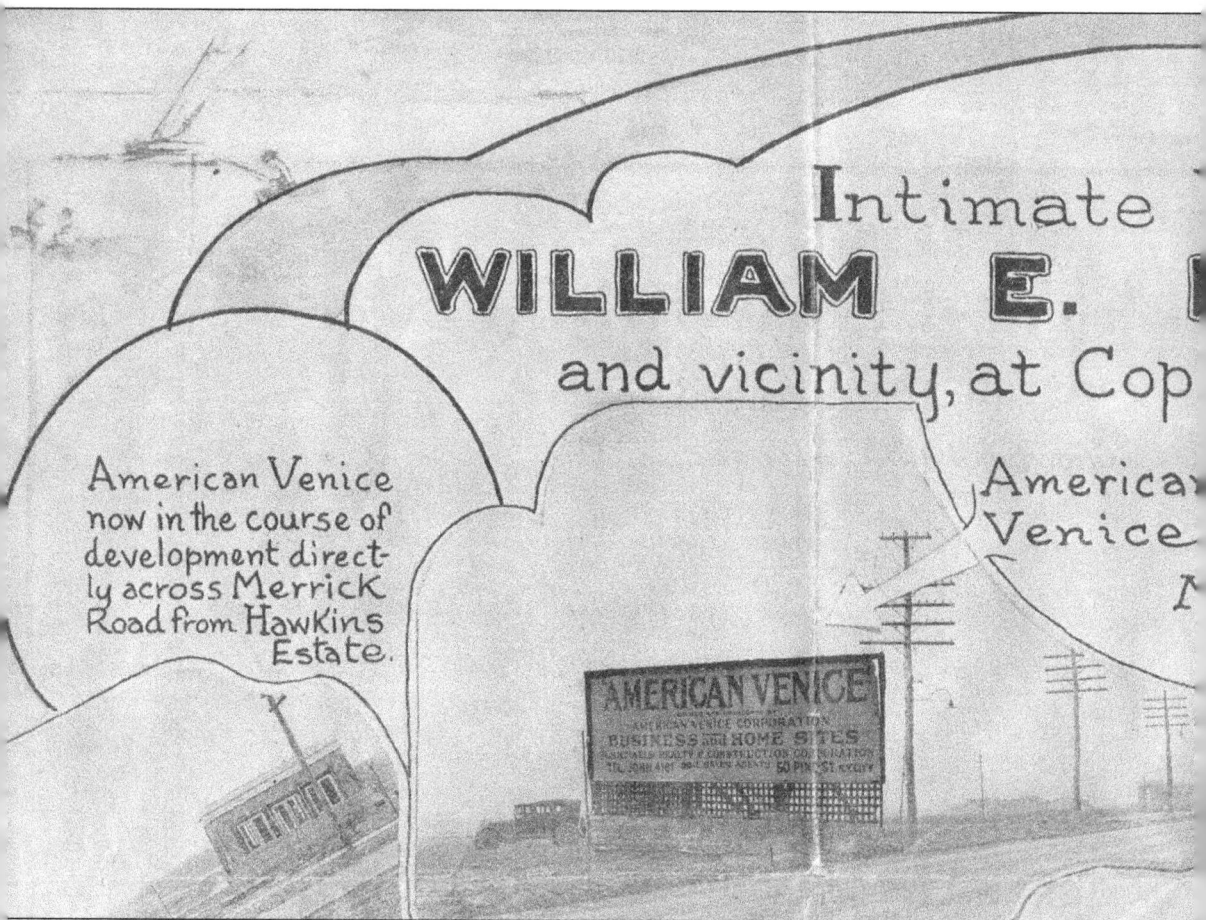

Intimate
WILLIAM E.
and vicinity, at Cop

American Venice
now in the course of
development direct-
ly across Merrick
Road from Hawkins
Estate.

Americar
Venice

AMERICAN VENICE
AMERICAN VENICE CORPORATION
BUSINESS and HOME SITES
MacDONALD REALTY & CONSTRUCTION CORPORATION
TEL. 50911-4191   SELLING AGENTS   50 PINE ST KO LIV

"Would you like to Spend the Day on a Millionaire's Estate?" inquired a 1926 advertisement for Copiague's Hawkins Estate. The Hawkins Estate neighborhood came about in the mid-1920s, around the same time as Amity Harbor, Deauville Gardens, and American Venice. The community was once the private family property of William E. Hawkins, president of the American Brass and Copper Company. This advertising broadside boasted the amenities of

vs of the

WKINS ESTATE

e and Lindenhurst, L.I.

Iawkins state

Hawkins Estate fronts on both sides of the Merrick Rd., opposite and ajoining American Venice.

Copiague's Hawkins Estate and, in particular, its proximity to the celebrated American Venice development. Other early advertisements for Hawkins Estate depicted Roaring Twenties bathing beauties with promises of luxurious, carefree recreation, including swimming, boating, and fishing, in a scenic environment.

A picturesque view of the palatial country residence owned by William E. Hawkins is seen here around the mid-1910s. The three-story gabled mansion was once visible from Montauk Highway, situated on a 176-acre parklike setting, which included a trout stream, horse stables, flower beds, fruit orchards, and vineyards. Reports indicated that the house would be used as the real estate company's administrative offices and a community center, along with the lake and park areas surrounding the building, for the new neighborhood. The Hawkins Estate development was advertised as being "in the highest state of cultivation . . . [and] the last word on a modern up-to-the-minute estate." Model homes built on the former estate property were equally promoted for their "modern" conveniences, such as kitchens "equipped with three cabinets, and ice box and various smaller compartments concealing or revealing the utilities of the housewife." (Calandrino-Natalie.)

The Hawkins Estate extended on both sides of Montauk Highway. The residential community that sprang forth from the millionaire's estate included a private bay beach for use by community residents. Cousins Nancy Biondi and Vilma Compani are pictured at the Hawkins beach around 1936. Many new Hawkins Estate homeowners limited their visits to the summer months; however, the following decades would bring more year-round residents. (Enz.)

By the late 1930s, the former Hawkins residence became the Nassau-Suffolk General Hospital. The wooden hospital suffered a couple of fires, including one in 1949 that was reportedly caused by the short circuit of an electric bulb near a patient using an oxygen mask. Firefighters from Copiague and three neighboring companies safely extinguished the blaze and evacuated 30 patients, including five newborns, to nearby private homes. (AHS.)

Additions were made to the three-story building, which was later renamed Lakeside Hospital. The hospital operated in Copiague until the 1970s. After its closure, the building was left vacant and succumbed to fire. The mansion-turned-medical center was eventually torn down and replaced by the Lakeside Manor apartment complex. (AHS.)

The influx of post–World War II residents to Copiague resulted in the launch and expansion of many businesses. The Copiague farmers' market on Sunrise Highway opened in the mid-1950s. The 12-acre property had a 500-foot-long building with booths offering a variety of goods from clothing to housewares and garden tools. (CW.)

The farmers' market fell victim to two fires during its brief tenure: April 28, 1958, and December 27, 1960. Both blazes were described as starting with a "mysterious explosion." A lack of water at the site plagued the firefighters from Copiague, Lindenhurst, Amityville, Babylon, and West Babylon, who came with 15 pieces of apparatus to battle 150-foot flames in the 1958 blaze. (AHS.)

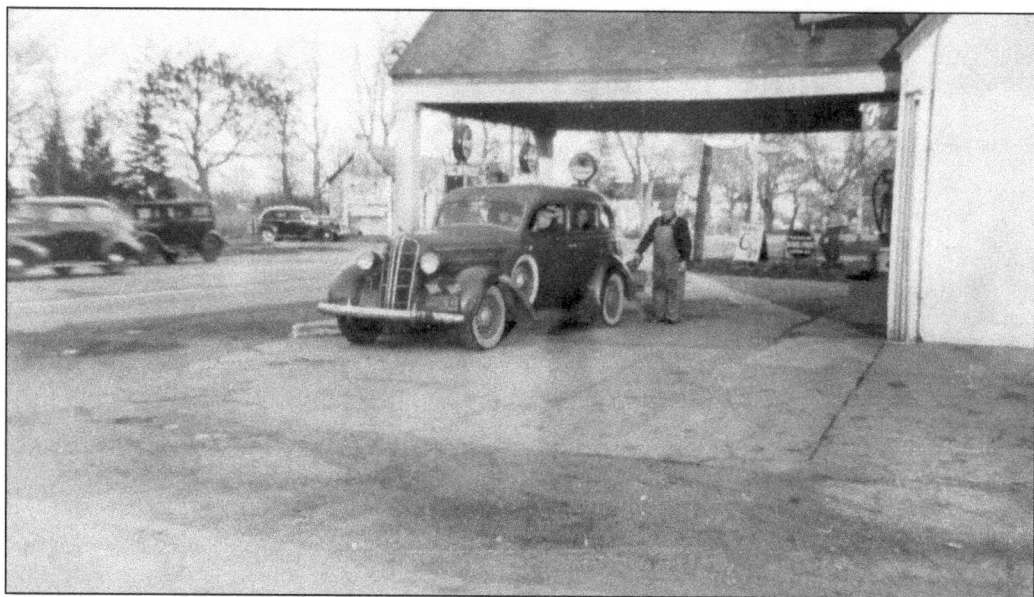

The Mobil gas station owned and operated by Marconiville residents Mr. and Mrs. Mastriani stood on the southeast corner of South Great Neck Road and Montauk Highway about 1936. Within a few decades from this photograph, along the country highway, Montauk Highway would become a bustling roadway. The gas station served the community until sometime around the 1970s. (Enz.)

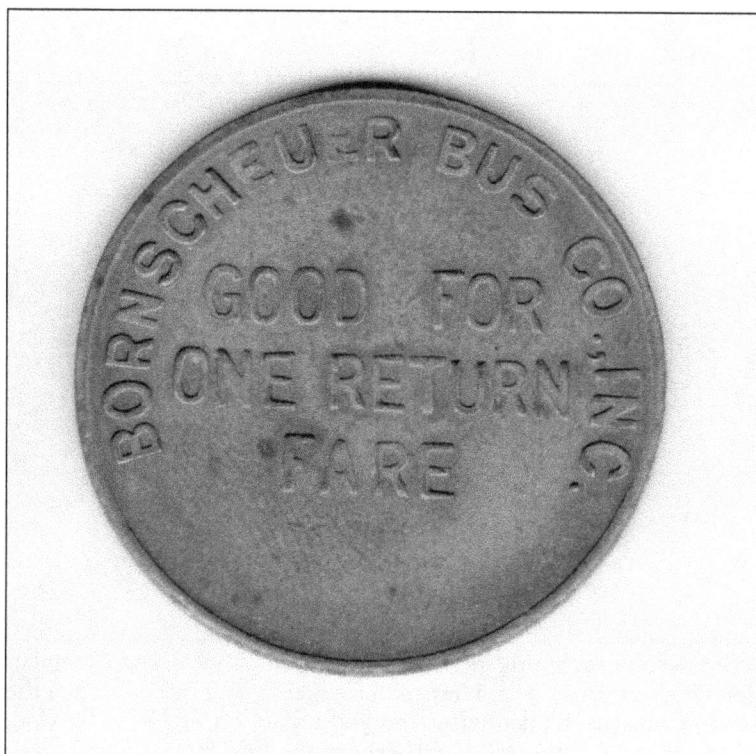

Shown here is a token for the Bornscheuer Bus Company from the late 1940s. Chester Bornscheuer started the bus route along Oak Street with service between Amityville and Babylon. Bornscheuer began with just one bus, which he drove himself, and later expanded to a second bus. The bus route continued until the mid- to late 1950s.

A postcard from the Old Landmark Inn, on Merrick Road, describes its fare as "Continental Specialties—Steaks—Chops—Long Island Duck—Lunch and Dinner Daily." The restaurant occupied the former residence and general store of James Teller Morris, who reportedly helped with the formation of the town of Babylon in 1872.

The All-Weather Roll 'n' Ice featured both ice-skating and roller-skating, on two separate levels, all year and was a popular fun spot. For just $2, including skate rental, ice skaters ($1.35 for roller skaters) could glide through an eventful evening. The skate house operated on the north side of Sunrise Highway, across the street from Johnny's All-Weather Drive-In.

The famous Johnny's All-Weather Drive-In opened on April 20, 1957, on the south side of Sunrise Highway between Bayview Avenue and Great Neck Road. The amenities of the popular drive-in included a children's playground, a caféteria, and a full-scale restaurant. A shuttle train was available to transport customers around the 28-acre site. (CW.)

The largest drive-in theater in New York State, Johnny's All-Weather Drive-In could accommodate 2,500 cars, in addition to its heated and air-conditioned indoor viewing area that seated 1,200 patrons. This view shows the rooftop seating area and a glimpse of the movie feature. The legendary drive-in closed its doors in 1984. (CW.)

Copiague's first post office was established in 1903, with Joseph C. Howell as postmaster. Shown here is the Copiague Post Office managed by postmaster Catharine L. Crollus from her family's grocery store on the east side of Great Neck Road between Oak Street and East Gate Avenue. Home mail delivery would not come for several decades, and many residents made daily trips to the post office to retrieve mail. (CPO.)

The Copiague Post Office dedication is seen here in 1955. Copiague's longest serving postmaster, Elbert H. Wild (at left), served nearly 30 years, from 1954 to 1983. At the podium is Stuyvesant Wainwright II, a member of the U.S. House of Representatives, New York's First Congressional District, 1953–1961. In 2004, the Copiague Post Office was dedicated as the Maxine S. Postal U.S. Post Office in honor of the Suffolk County legislator who passed away that year. (AHS.)

The Copiague Union School band parades south on Great Neck Road past the old Copiague Pharmacy at the northeast corner of Oak Street in the early 1950s. The students are led by band director James Bradis (at right) who later became the assistant principal of the junior-senior high school. The Copiague Pharmacy building is presently known as the Prisco Building. (Cahaney.)

A parade marches south past Bohack Grocery around 1957. Bohack's store stood on the northeast corner of Great Neck Road and Oak Street and was a popular local grocery store chain. The Copiague store closed in the early 1970s, though the company continued for a few more years before closing its business in 1977. (VFW.)

Six

PUBLIC EDUCATION

The Copiague Union School, now known as the Great Neck Road Elementary School, is seen as it appeared on the school district's letterhead in 1935. At that time, the Copiague Union School was the community's only school, educating students from kindergarten through eighth grade. The Copiague School District operated a single school from the 1800s until 1950, when the neighboring Scudder Avenue Elementary School was opened. (CSD.)

Students posed in front of their modest country school on June 30, 1899. The school was located on the north side of South Country Road, now Montauk Highway, just west of Great Neck Road. This schoolhouse was purportedly built in 1889, the same year that a bell was donated to the school, which was then known as the East Amityville School. (AHS.)

A teacher in Rhinebeck, New York, and former Copiague student, Susan C. Morris donated a bronze bell to the school on December 26, 1889. Morris's father owned a general store where the Old Landmark Inn was later built. Fashioned by the Meneely Bell Company of Troy, New York, the bell beckoned several generations of students to school before it was retired to this pedestal in front of the Great Neck Road Elementary School.

An interior view of the East Amityville School and its sole teacher, Miss Zufeldt, are shown here in 1898. This was Zufeldt's first year as teacher of the East Amityville School. All students from grades equivalent to kindergarten through sixth grade were taught by just one teacher in the one-room schoolhouse. On the wall behind her desk hangs an abacus and a primary reading exercise titled "My dog is on the log." School board minutes indicated that the previous year, 1897, the school's enrollment was 60 students, that the schoolhouse had been assessed at $1,000, and that the school library had 133 books valued at approximately $25. Around 1901, the entire school building was relocated north to Great Neck Road, which was a more central location for the school district. The community's first public schoolhouse was a one-room structure reportedly built in 1802 along Montauk Highway. (AHS.)

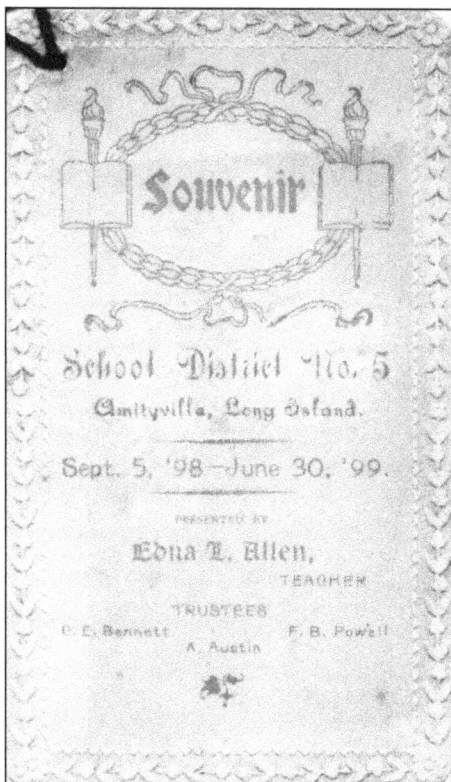

This is an image of a decorative souvenir card for School District No. 5 from the 1898–1899 school year. The other name for School District No. 5 was the East Amityville School, which later became the Copiague Union School. That year, the 39 students enrolled at the school were under the tutelage of teacher Edna L. Allen. (AHS.)

Eventually the community's growing population necessitated a larger schoolhouse. On July 18, 1910, the school board accepted the proposal of architect Edward P. Gelf for a wood-frame schoolhouse at a "cost [of] $9300 with two rooms furnished and $9800 with four rooms furnished. Architects fees $350 additional." Construction commenced in July 1911, and the new school opened during the 1911–1912 school year. The Copiague Union Chapel is seen at right.

In December 1911, the *Amityville Record* reported, "The new school building in Copiague will have a handsome new American flag to float over it." The flag came as a gift from Eagle Council No. 45, Junior Order Unified American Mechanics. The school population continued to rise, due in part to the popularity of the nearby Marconiville community. Copiague students are pictured against the background of the school in 1918. (CSD.)

Students pose in their classroom at the wooden schoolhouse in 1919. In 1920, the school board considered an extension to the school. Overcrowding in the school required kindergarten classes to be held in the nearby Copiague Union Chapel on Scudder Avenue. The most pressing issues faced by the overcapacity school were the lack of fire escapes and only two outhouses for use by the students and faculty. (CSD.)

In 1924, the school board voted an appropriation of $70,000 for a brick extension to the wooden building, providing fire escape access, four new classrooms, a 350-seat auditorium, and a modern restroom. The plans of Amityville architect Lewis Inglee were approved by the board, and construction by Pearce Brothers of New York began in spring 1925. From Great Neck Road, the old wooden structure would have been eclipsed from view, shadowed by the modern brick extension, but it remained an integral part of the school for decades more. Attached to the face of the original structure, students passed seamlessly between classes in the old wooden school and the brick addition. In 1930, Inglee was called upon again to add six new classrooms, a modern kindergarten room, a school office, and a board meeting room to the 1925 brick addition. The extension included a northern entryway inscribed "Boys" and one along Scudder Avenue for "Girls," though such gender separation was reportedly not enforced. The boys' entrance was later enshrouded in another extension, while the girls' demarcation remains. (AHS.)

In 1953, a final extension was made to the northern end of the school. The expansion added classrooms as well as a large gymnasium and modern caféteria. The original 1911 wooden portion of the school was replaced by an eight-classroom brick wing in 1959. (AHS.)

Pictured in 2009, the Great Neck Road Elementary School has a yearly enrollment of approximately 500 students, kindergarten through fifth grade. It is the oldest elementary school in the town of Babylon, serving students since 1911. Although an interior plaque states, "Copiague Grade School—Erected 1931," the commemorative plaque does not take into account the original 1911 portion of the school and the 1926 expansion. (Rodi.)

To relieve congestion at the Great Neck Road School, in 1950 an 18-room building was leased on Scudder Avenue, and it became known as the "Annex Building." Later named the Scudder Avenue School, the school building was originally designed for use as a factory, though it was never used as such. Shown is an architect's model of the school complex. (AHS.)

An elementary class at the Scudder Avenue School gathered for this photograph around 1956. The Scudder Avenue School had a total of 22 classrooms with cement floors and walls made of beaverboard. Former school principal Elizabeth Eide recalled that the cement floors kicked up so much dirt that the teachers went home with "dirty ankles." (Enz.)

The local Reds Little League baseball team posed in front of the Scudder Avenue School around 1956. In 1954, a brick structure was added to the school site. A few years later, the school was expanded to include a gymnasium and caféteria. The original corrugated metal factory building was removed in 1964. (Enz.)

As a result of the decreased school population, the Scudder Avenue School was closed in 1979. In 1985, the old school building was demolished and replaced by the Cambridge Square Apartments. Mere minutes before its destruction, the building's dedication plaque was rescued by Ralph Soluri and now hangs in the offices of the *Copiague Weekly* newspaper.

Deauville Gardens Elementary School is seen here during construction about 1957. The building was designed by architects Knappe and Johnson and built by Jonwal Construction Company, Inc. The Knappe and Johnson firm also designed the Copiague Middle School and the Babylon Town Hall on Sunrise Highway, which all opened in the same year, 1958.

The Deauville Gardens Elementary School was expanded just a few years after its opening, adding 16 new rooms and a caféteria area. With nearly 1,000 students spanning from kindergarten through fifth grade, it is the largest elementary school in Copiague. Located on Deauville Boulevard, the sprawling school took its name from the 1920s real estate development Deauville Gardens, near the western border of Copiague.

Susan E. Wiley (second row, center) was born in Amityville in 1902. A graduate of Harriet Melissa Mills Teachers College, Wiley taught at the Copiague Union School from 1925 until her death in 1952. The year before her death, Wiley was honored for her years of teaching with a testimonial dinner. The revered Miss Wiley was also a six-year president of the Copiague PTA and a Girl Scout leader. (Vacca.)

In 1963, a fourth Copiague elementary school was opened, situated on Scudder Avenue between the Great Neck Road School and the Scudder Avenue School. The new school was named in honor of the beloved Susan E. Wiley, who taught school in Copiague for 27 years. Pictured in 2009, the school educates an average of 750 students.

Copiague High School

This 1961 graduation invitation for the Copiague Junior-Senior High School depicts the new school in pen and ink. Prior to the erection of this new school, Copiague students who wished to continue their education through the 12th grade had to attend high schools in other neighboring districts. Most Copiague students chose to attend the high schools in either Lindenhurst or Amityville. (VFW.)

The present Copiague Middle School is located on the east side of Great Neck Road, just south of Sunrise Highway. The school presently educates nearly 1,200 students in the sixth, seventh, and eighth grades. With the erection of the Copiague High School in 1966–1967, the former junior-senior high school became the junior high school and later the Copiague Middle School.

Walter G. O'Connell's Copiague career began in 1950 as an English teacher at the Copiague Union School. O'Connell became principal of the elementary school in 1953, as shown above. He became the first principal of the new junior-senior high school in 1958 and the first high school principal in 1967. O'Connell officially retired as principal in 1971 but continued teaching through the 1980s. In 1999, Trouville Road was dedicated in his honor. (O'Connell.)

A new senior high school was opened in 1967 on Dixon Avenue, with Walter G. O'Connell serving as its first principal. Commemorating his long-standing and unwavering dedication to the education of all Copiague children, the Copiague High School was renamed the Walter G. O'Connell Copiague High School in his honor in 2000. The school presently educates over 1,500 students from grades nine through 12.

Copiague's high school has a strong tradition of competitive teams and players. Winning the 2009 New York State Class AA Championship, the girls' varsity basketball team, shown here with school administration and coaches, became the first Copiague team to win a state championship. From 1958 to 2008, the boys' varsity basketball program has won a total of 20 league, three large school, two Suffolk County, and one Long Island championships. (CSD.)

The Walter G. O'Connell Copiague High School marching band was invited to perform at the 2008 Macy's Thanksgiving Day Parade in New York City. First formed in 1984, the Copiague High School marching band has earned 16 championship titles and more than 600 awards, citations, and proclamations since 1991. (CSD.)

Seven

COMMUNITY SERVICE

Copiague's Honor Roll, erected in 1944, was dedicated to Copiague residents who died in military service. During World War II, the names of local servicemen and women were inscribed thereon. Pictured at the north end of the Copiague Union School along Great Neck Road, the base of the memorial was moved south to the corner of Scudder Avenue when the school building was expanded in the early 1950s. (Cahaney.)

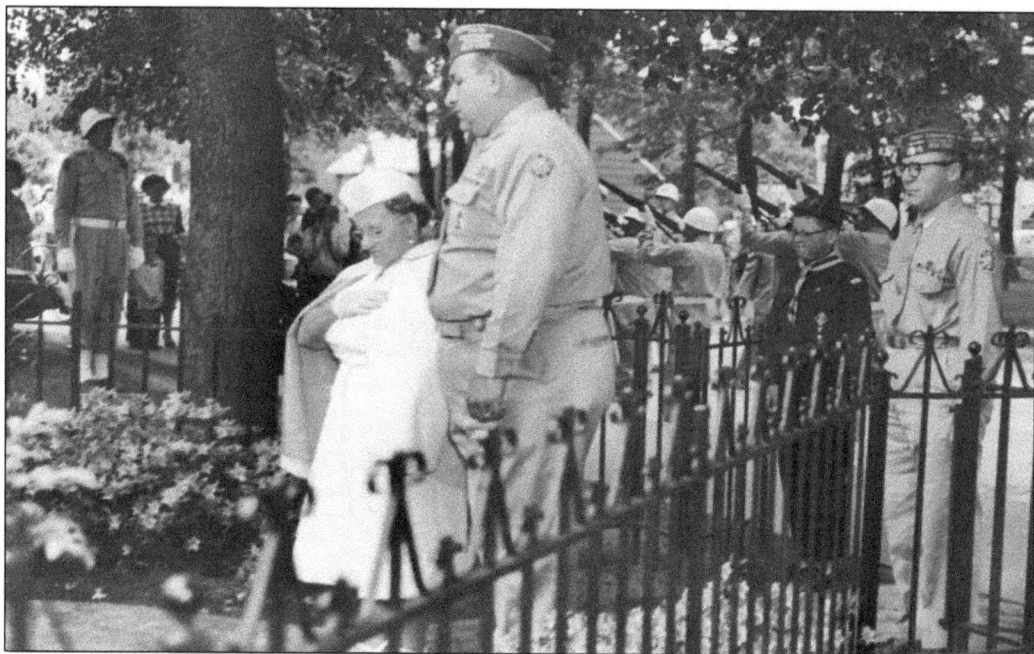

Members of the Copiague Veterans of Foreign Wars Warren Keer Post No. 9482 paid tribute to their fellow servicemen and women with ceremonies following a Memorial Day parade at the veterans' memorial, located on the northwest corner of Great Neck Road and Scudder Avenue. VFW members fired a memorial salute in the background. (VFW.)

The veterans' memorial pictured in 2009 in front of the Great Neck Road Elementary School was first erected to honor service personnel in World War II. The monument has been revised and "Dedicated to the Men and Women of Copiague who served in World War I—World War II—Korean Action—Vietnam—Persian Gulf—Iraq—Afghanistan."

The memorial to veterans of World War I situated on the southeast corner of Great Neck Road and Marconi Boulevard was commissioned by Marconiville founder John Campagnoli. The inset of the memorial stone was first mounted on Campagnoli's property and later moved to the present site. The stone, which is inscribed "Their Adopted Country Found Them Ready," lists Marconiville residents who served in World War I. (Rodi.)

The Veterans of Foreign Wars Warren Keer Post No. 9482 on Trouville Road was formed in 1952 with 59 members. The post's charter states that members "served honorably in the Army, Navy or Marine Corps of the United States of America in foreign wars of the United States of America." (Rodi.)

Members of the Veterans of Foreign Wars Warren Keer Post No. 9482 march south on Great Neck Road near Oak Street on Memorial Day about 1957. Great Neck Road, extending from Route 110 north to south of Montauk Highway, is a main travel artery through Copiague. (VFW.)

Veterans of Foreign Wars Warren Keer Post No. 9482 established the first Boy Scout troop in Copiague—Pack No. 154—in 1954, pictured here around the time of their formation. Post No. 9482 continues its sponsorship of Pack No. 154, which remains active in the Copiague community to the present day. (VFW.)

Community leaders, veterans, and students gathered at the north end of the Copiague Union School for a Memorial Day program led by the American Legion (at center) around 1950. Placement of the veterans' memorial at the Copiague Union School, later the Great Neck Road School, made it an appropriate location for the community's Memorial Day activities. (Cahaney.)

American Legion Post No. 1105 relocated from Amityville to Elm Street in Copiague. At the post, a monument honors four World War II chaplains—Lt. John P. Washington, Catholic; Lt. Alexander D. Goode, Jewish; Lt. George L. Fox, Protestant; and Lt. Clark V. Poling, Protestant—"who gave their life jackets that four soldiers might live. The S.S. *Dorchester* was torpedoed February 3, 1943. As it sank the four were seen linked arm in arm, heads uplifted in prayer." (Rodi.)

VIGILANT ENGINE CO., DIXON AVE. & GR. NECK RD., COPIAGUE, N. Y.

Prior to the establishment of the Copiague Fire District, fire protection for the community was purchased from neighboring districts Amityville and Lindenhurst. On July 15, 1927, a citizens group gathered at the Hawkins Estate clubhouse to discuss fire protection for Copiague. The group petitioned the Babylon Town Board, under supervisor Joseph P. Warta, and a charter was granted on December 9, 1927. (Cahaney.)

In its first year of operation, 1928, the new Copiague Fire Department built two firehouses, one on the south side and one on north. The northern firehouse, on the northwest corner of Dixon Avenue and Great Neck Road, was operated by the Vigilant Engine Company whose original apparatus consisted of a 500-gallon-per-minute LaFrance pumper and a LaFrance hose truck, pictured here c. 1954. (CFD.)

96

FIRE DEPARTMENT - COPIAGUE, L. I.

The fire department headquarters was built farther south on Great Neck Road, a short distance from Montauk Highway, and was managed by the Southside Fire Company, which changed its name to Eagle Engine Company at their first official meeting. A four-tank chemical truck and a city service ladder truck, both made by LaFrance, were the first apparatus assigned to Eagle Engine Company. (AHS.)

In November 1928, the Copiague Fire Department officially assumed responsibility for all fire protection in the new district. Thomas Henry, who later became a Town of Babylon councilman, was named the first chief of the Copiague Fire Department. The department's first major call was to a pants factory fire in February 1929, which spread to a neighboring butcher shop, barbershop, tailor, and ice cream parlor. (CFD.)

97

Joe Dellavecchia, one of the Copiague Fire Department's founding members, drives the Vigilant Engine Company's original 1928 LaFrance pumper truck. In 1962, a local newspaper reported that the pumper had been rebuilt, could operate to modern standards, and was one of the oldest working fire engines in Suffolk County. The historical truck, restored in its original red, is still used for parades and ceremonies. (CFD.)

Rapid growth of the Copiague community necessitated the formation of the fire police squad in 1937, which was assigned to control increased vehicular traffic at fire scenes. Citing the growing problem, in 1939 the New York State Legislature established fire police organizations as part of fire departments. The Copiague Fire Police Squad was disbanded by the 1980s. (CFD.)

Members of the Vigilant Engine Company, from the Copiague Fire Station on Dixon Avenue, were the first responders to this local house fire in the early 1990s. Vigilant Engine Company members Bill Ketchem and Louie Demino are seen atop the fire engine, with Demino operating the deck gun toward the blaze. (CFD.)

Keeping abreast in skills and training to provide Copiague citizens the absolute best in fire and rescue services, the Copiague Firematic Drill Team excels in competition. Competing as the Yellow Birds, the Copiague Drill Team won the 2009 New York State Old Fashioned Drill, in which the exercises are performed without the aid of motorized equipment, just buckets, hoses, ladders, and hand-pulled carts. (CFD.)

The fleet of the Copiague Fire Department was under the direction of Chief Vernon Carpenter in 1961. In addition to the chief's car, shown in front, the 1961 fleet consisted of four pumper trucks, which form the second row. In the back, from left to right, are the department's equipment truck, ladder truck, and ambulance. (CFD.)

The fleet of the Copiague Fire Department is pictured at Tanner Park along the shores of the Great South Bay in 1992. The modern fleet includes an aerial ladder truck, pumper trucks, a heavy rescue truck, three ambulances, and a boat for marine search and rescue. In addition to the Vigilant and Eagle Engine Companies, the fire department also includes the Hook Ladder Company and a rescue squad. (CFD.)

The present Station No. 1 of the Copiague Fire Department is located near the southeast corner of Dixon Avenue and Great Neck Road. This north end fire station was dedicated in 1954, replacing the original station that stood across the street at the northwestern corner of the intersection. In 2010, the station supports a crew of 40 volunteer firefighters.

The Copiague Fire Department built a new headquarters just north of its original, and it was dedicated in May 1966. In its first year of service, 1929, the Copiague Fire Department had four fire trucks and responded to 18 calls. In their 50th year, 1978, the department had 10 trucks and averaged 110 calls per month. In 2009, the department responded to approximately 600 general calls and 1,680 rescue calls. (Rodi.)

The earliest law enforcement agents in Copiague and the Town of Babylon were four constables, each assigned to patrol a quadrant of the town. Around 1905, constables were provided with motorcycles. Pictured here are the Babylon town constables on "Electrification Day," May 25, 1925, when the first electric Long Island Rail Road train ran on the Babylon branch. (SPM.)

The Town of Babylon Police Department formed in 1947 and was headquartered at Babylon Town Hall on Main Street in the village of Babylon. Town police officers took over the duties previously held by town constables. Town police officer Peter Smith was assigned to Copiague, Car 27. In 1960, the town police department merged into the new Suffolk County Police Department, and the Copiague sector became Car 107, as it remains today. (Cahaney.)

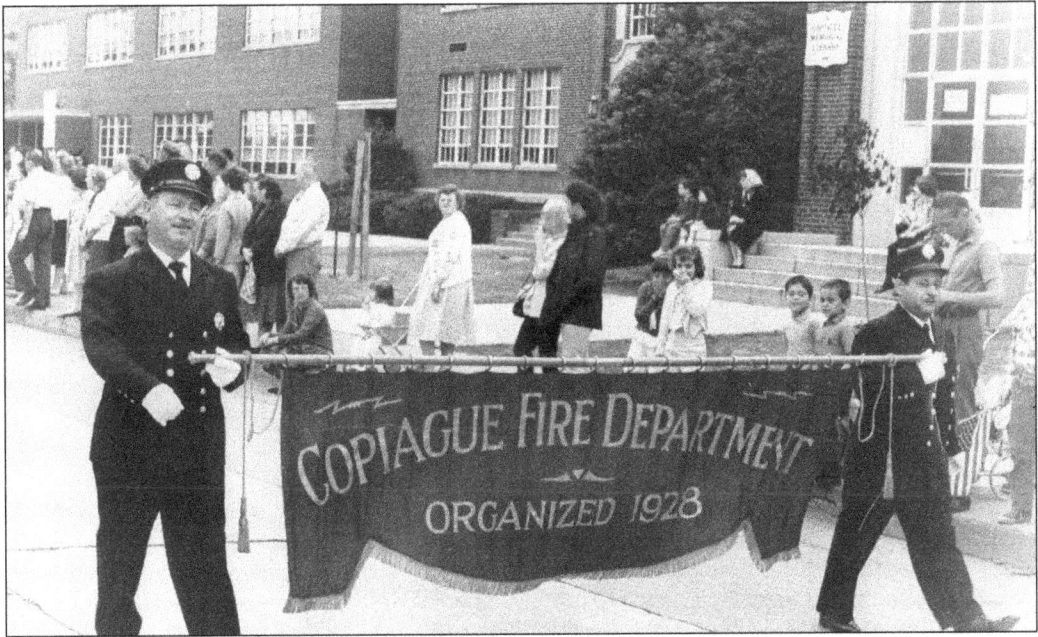

The Copiague Memorial Public Library had its start in one room of the Great Neck Road Elementary School in 1960. The library was opened without a single book, but volunteers swiftly collected over 4,000 books within a few months. The library entrance is seen in the back right of this parade photograph, with a sign hanging to the left of the door that with the name "Copiague Memorial Library." (CFD.)

Less than a decade after its opening, the library was ready to expand. The library relocated a half-mile south on Great Neck Road to the old Copiague Fire Department headquarters. The new two-story library was officially opened in October 1969. With 4,500 square feet of space, the library offered over 24,000 items for its 9,500 patrons. (Cahaney.)

After two decades in the renovated fire station, the library took occupancy of a new custom-designed building on Deauville Boulevard in November 1989. The library was officially dedicated the following May. The library has come a long way since its modest beginning. In fall 2009, Copiague residents approved a building expansion, adding 3,000 square feet to the interior of the existing structure.

The relinquished fire department–turned–public library was revitalized yet again in 2004, when the building was refurbished as the Polish and Slavic Federal Credit Union. Originally formed in 1976 as the Industrial and Trade Federal Credit Union, the Fairfield, New Jersey–based Polish and Slavic Federal Credit Union lays claim as the largest ethnic credit union in the United States.

The Kiwanis Club of Copiague was formed in the 1980s. In fall of 2009, the Kiwanis Club was joined by Boy Scout Troop 284, the high school Key Club, the middle school Builders Club, and school administrators to erect this patriotic Field of Honor in front of the Copiague Middle School, consisting of 100 American flags paying homage to veterans, past and present. (Rodi.)

The stately clock at the southeast corner of Great Neck Road and Oak Street was erected by the Copiague Chamber of Commerce, who also maintains the Merchants Plaza site. Organized in the 1950s, the Copiague Chamber of Commerce has incorporated this clock image in their logo. The chamber is comprised of local businesses, residents, and organizations "determined to improve the quality of life and general business environment in Copiague." (Rodi.)

The Copiague Beautification Society was formed by a group of local residents in 1997. In conjunction with Suffolk County and the Town of Babylon Community Development Program, as well as the support of local elected officials, the Beautification Society has helped to organize volunteers and fundraising efforts for landscape enhancement projects that adorn the Copiague community, such as this attractive display for the Hawkins Estate at Hawkins Boulevard and Montauk Highway. (Rodi.)

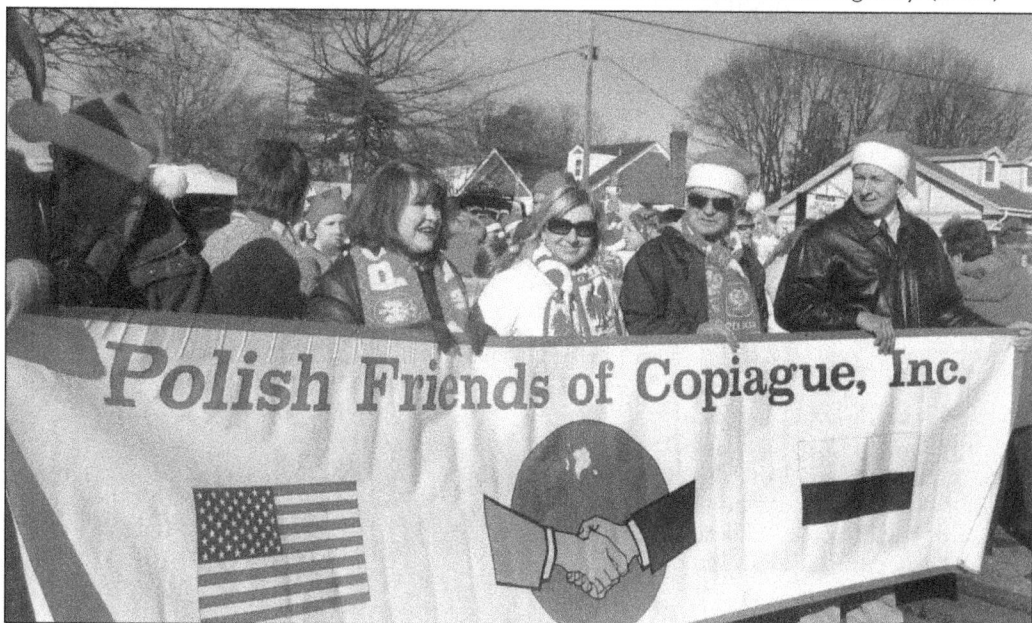

Members of the Polish Friends of Copiague are shown at the annual Christmas parade. Reflecting the growing population of Polish descent in Copiague, Polish Friends was founded in 1994. The charity organization promotes educational and informational activities for people of all ages. Working with the Parish Counsel of Our Lady of the Assumption Catholic Church, the organization supports Long Island Polish schools and people in life-crisis situations. (PFoC.)

Eight

RELIGIOUS INSTITUTIONS

Copiague is home to Bethel African Methodist Episcopal (AME) Church, celebrated as Long Island's oldest black church. In 1814, the Bethel Sunday school was started in Amityville by Daniel Squires and Delancy H. Miller. The following year, they organized the church and held services in members' homes as the congregation grew. Bethel's first pastor, Benjamin Bates, traveled from Jamaica on foot each week until the church members were able to give him a horse.

After years of temporary facilities, in 1850 the burgeoning congregation built their first permanent structure at the northwest corner of Jefferson and Albany Avenues on property donated by Elias Hunter. In 1866, the church joined the AME Church. The AME Church was created in Philadelphia in 1787 from the Free African Society, which protested slavery and the dehumanization of all African people.

Alma Mosley painted this image of the old Bethel AME Church on Albany Avenue, which was enhanced with several modifications. Around 1900, the building was raised for the addition of a lower auditorium. Additions were made in 1940 and again in 1957. Despite the expansions made, the thriving church lacked ample space to serve its church community, and the church leadership sought new opportunities to enlarge the church.

The decision to relocate the church to Simmons Street in Copiague was one not taken lightly by the congregation. On June 28, 1962, groundbreaking ceremonies took place for the new house of worship. The main sanctuary was ready for services held on Palm Sunday, March 19, 1967, using folding chairs and a donated pulpit.

Although the church relocated to Copiague, the old Amityville church remained a special place for the church members. A committee was formed for the restoration of the old church and to secure landmark status for the building; however, the historical building succumbed to fire in 1989. Fortunately, the cornerstone, bell, and cross had been moved from the old church and placed in the vestibule of the new church in 1974.

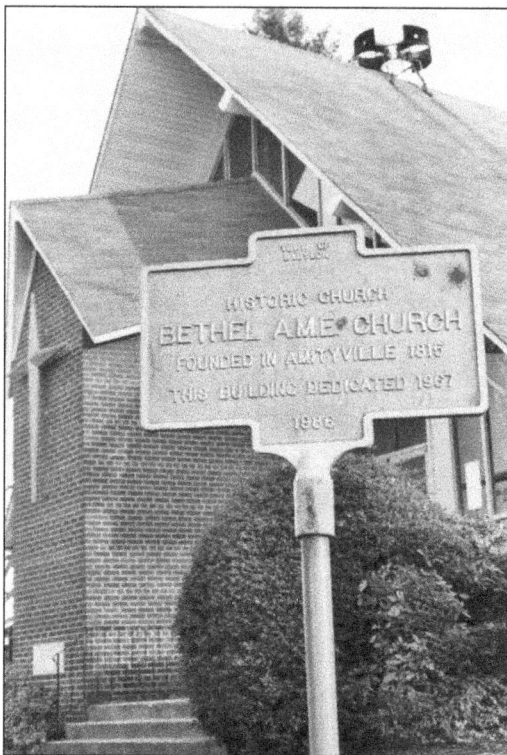

On January 19, 1986, the Town of Babylon Historic Preservation Commission dedicated a cast-iron historical marker, which was placed in front of the church on Simmons Street. The historical Bethel AME Church, whose history spans the communities of Copiague and Amityville and which boasts a congregation of over 600 members, will celebrate its bicentennial anniversary in 2015. (Rodi.)

The history of the Full Gospel Christian Church began in 1931, when Vincenzo Gorgolione and his family moved to Copiague, opening their home for prayer meetings. By the mid-1930s, the growing group rented a storefront on Oak Street. A decade later, church member Sabina Marvella and her husband donated property for the first permanent church. (FGCC.)

The members elected to borrow $2,500 to erect their first church, a 1,500-square-foot building accommodating 70 people. Located on Great Neck Road, just south of the present Sunrise Highway, some residents questioned the placement of the church in such a remote location; however, the area around the church has since become one of the busiest areas in the community. (FGCC.)

The dedication of the new church building was held in August 1946. It was named the Italian Pentecostal Church of Copiague, with the main services held in Italian. As membership grew, the predominant language changed to English, and in 1959, the group reincorporated as the Full Gospel Christian Church. In 1981, the church began a Spanish-speaking congregation, which has continued since that time, to serve the growing community. (FGCC.)

The small church was expanded in 1968 and again in 1981, with much of the construction completed by its own members. The original sanctuary structure is seen at right. In 1983, the Copiague Christian Academy was started for the education of preschool and elementary students; it continues as a preschool. (Rodi.)

COPIAGUE UNION CHURCH, SCUDDER AVE., COPIAGUE, N. Y.

This is a 1930s postcard view of the Copiague Union Church on Scudder Avenue, located east of Great Neck Road. The Copiague Union Church, a nondenominational house of worship, was founded in 1896 and is believed to be the oldest church building in Copiague. Scudder Avenue was named for Scudder Jervis, whose family attended the Copiague Union Church and lived just south of the namesake street.

112

The exterior of the church building has had few changes. It is the same chapel pictured behind the wooden Copiague Union School on page 80. The former Copiague Union Church was purchased in 1991 by the congregation of Calvary Chapel of Nassau County, which originated in Hicksville, New York. The church is now the Christ Covenant Church, a member of the Confederation of Reformed Evangelical Churches. (Rodi.)

Seen here is St. John's Baptist Church, located on Bethpage Road, just north of Sunrise Highway. Modern residents may question why there are two non-connecting streets named Bethpage Road in Copiague: Prior to the erection of the middle school and high school, located just south of Sunrise Highway, both streets named Bethpage Road were connected between Great Neck Road and Dixon Avenue. (Rodi.)

Zion Gospel Church, located at 90 Warren Street, was founded in 1949 by four women pioneers: Rev. Mother Christine Gomez, Rev. Trifosia Evora, Rev. Maude Smith, and missionary Mattie Pierce. The women sold their New York City home to start their missionary outreach in Amityville-Copiague. The first completed church measured approximately 25 feet by 30 feet, as shown here in 1951. (Zion Gospel.)

To accommodate the growing congregation, Zion Gospel Church was extended in 1958 and in 1976. The last enlargement to the building was in 1988. Zion Gospel Church has a long history as a multicultural, multigenerational, and family-oriented congregation. Present-day pastors Elder Willard Price III and Rev. Clementine R. Price are products of the church's founders' dedicated outreach to the community. (Zion Gospel.)

A modern-day view of the Copiague Christian Church on Pinelawn Avenue is shown here. The property was purchased in 1953 for $3,800 by the United Christian Church of Copiague, who built and expanded the church over several years. By 1997, membership in the United Christian Church of Copiague dwindled, and the church was donated in 1998 to the newly formed Copiague Christian Church, which was a branch of the Farmingdale Christian Church. (Rodi.)

A springtime, outdoor procession of parishioners of Copiague's Our Lady of the Assumption Church is pictured here. The church was formed by Copiague residents in 1927, and construction of a church began two years later. Before that time, the closest Catholic parishes to Copiague-Marconiville were St. Martin of Tours, in Amityville, and Our Lady of Perpetual Help, in Lindenhurst. (VBHPS.)

John Campagnoli, founder of the Marconiville community, donated the land for the new church. In 1929, construction of the foundation and basement for the new sanctuary began, but it would be 10 more years until the main floor was completed, around 1942. During the construction years, parishioners held services in the underground portion of the structure. (AHS.)

A 1948 view of the Our Lady of the Assumption auditorium is pictured here. Originally dedicated as the Copiague Community Center, popular activities at the hall included roller-skating, live opera performances, and professional boxing and wrestling. Gene Stanlee "Mr. America" and Antonino "Argentine" Rocca were some of the popular wrestlers who made appearances in Copiague. The center was also the home of the Catholic Youth Organization and the semipro Mustangs basketball team. (AHS.)

OUR LADY OF THE ASSUMPTION MEMORIAL SHRINE, MOLLOY ST., COPIAGUE, N. Y.

Photography by Bourda Studio, Oak St., Copiague, N. Y. — Tel. Amityville 1548

The Our Lady of the Assumption Memorial Shrine was constructed south of the church sanctuary by the parish priest Fr. Francis DelVecchio, Fr. Frank Cannizzaro, and the Pagliarulo Brothers construction company around the late 1940s. The concrete shrine bore a resemblance to the outstretched wings of an airplane, as a tribute to U.S. military personnel. During World War II, photographs of local servicemen were displayed in an area beneath the shrine. (Cahaney.)

Within the shrine are a number of memorial plaques, including "For God and Country—Our Lady of the Assumption Shrine Dedicated to Our War Heroes." The shrine has been renovated since its construction but remains a tranquil and meditative spot with commemorative plaques and benches for local residents. East of the shrine, a memorial was erected and dedicated to Joseph "Pepi" Cardino (1932–2005) by his family. (Rodi.)

Our Lady of the Assumption church and rectory is pictured in 2009. The church originated with many Italian-speaking residents and those of Italian descent, with services offered in English and Italian. In response to the influx of Spanish-speaking and Polish-speaking residents, the church offers weekly services to church members in their native languages. (Rodi.)

Nine

COPIAGUE IN THE 21ST CENTURY

The Copiague community has been many things to many people—a place to work, learn, serve, live, and play. For generations of residents, the area has lived up to its Native American moniker as a "sheltered harbor." While its historic legacy is renowned, the Copiague community of the 21st century is just beginning to write its own story. (Rodi.)

Copiague goes forth into the 21st century as an ever-growing and adapting community for residents and business owners. Plans have been proposed for the revitalization of the Great Neck Road downtown area and other areas. On December 23, 2009, community members led by Babylon town supervisor Steve Bellone dedicated new decorative streetlights along Montauk Highway in memory of lifelong Copiague resident Joseph Costantino. (CW.)

A popular activity for generations of children, the Copiague Youth League began with baseball teams in 1958 and soon added basketball to its programs. Soccer was added in the 1980s and lacrosse in 2000. Little Conference Football and Cheerleading, which started in 1965, merged with the Copiague Youth League in 1990. As of 2010, the Copiague Youth League supports sports programs for approximately 1,200 local kids. (CYL.)

Published since fall of 2007, the *Copiague Weekly* newspaper has become a weekly anticipation for the Copiague community, reporting and promoting local events and businesses. For decades, news about Copiague was limited to arbitrary reports in newspapers of neighboring communities, with the exception of the *Copiague Journal*, which was briefly published in the 1950s. (CW.)

Copiague is one of 10 hamlets in the town of Babylon. The town of Babylon has nine other hamlets—Deer Park, East Farmingdale, North Amityville, North Babylon, North Lindenhurst, West Babylon, Wheatley Heights, and Wyandanch as well as the barrier beach communities—and the three incorporated villages of Amityville, Babylon, and Lindenhurst. The local seat of government is the Babylon Town Hall, located on Sunrise Highway in nearby North Lindenhurst. (Gravano.)

The town of Babylon, the fifth-most-populous town in the state of New York, is governed by the Babylon Town Board, pictured in 2010 from left to right: councilman Antonio A. Martinez, councilwoman and deputy supervisor Ellen T. McVeety, town supervisor Steven Bellone, councilwoman and Copiague resident Jacqueline A. Gordon, and councilman Lindsay P. Henry. (Gravano.)

Richard "Dick" Tanner, general foreman of the Town of Babylon Highway Department, and Arthur M. Cromarty, Babylon town supervisor (1958–1963), surveyed the 93-acre Copiague Park site around 1962. The Copiague Park, which hugs the shore of the Great South Bay, was later named in honor of Tanner, who resided in Copiague.

Richard Tanner was born in Brooklyn on August 2, 1895. As an adult, he moved to Copiague and became active in community affairs. He was a member of the Copiague Fire Department and the Suffolk County Republican Committee for over 20 years and served on the Copiague Board of Education for eight years. (AHS.)

The pavilion along the beach at Tanner Park is shown as it appeared in 1958. As pictured behind the pavilion, Tanner Park was largely undeveloped at that time. In the decades that followed, many improvements and additions have been made to the parkland, which today includes multiple sports fields, an amphitheater, a spray park, a skateboard park, and training facilities for the Copiague Fire Department's drill team.

The Tanner Park pavilion was built in 2008. The building's solar panels reflect the town's energy-saving initiatives. That same year, a band shell was constructed on the west side of the park pavilion. The open-air performance stage hosts concerts in the summer months. The Tanner Park is also the site of a community senior center. (Gravano.)

Designed for residents of all ages, a children's tree house–themed spray park opened in 2007, adjacent to the public bathing beach. The parkland was formerly part of the mid-1920s Amity Harbor community developed by George Brown. In the 1930s, Brown reportedly relinquished the property to satisfy unpaid property taxes. The uncultivated tract remained untouched for decades until the Town of Babylon developed it as a community park. (Gravano.)

Tanner Park is the largest of more than 29 parks and beaches operated by the Town of Babylon. In 2004, a skateboard area was added. The following year, the skate park was renamed in honor of longtime Copiague resident Marcia Curcio. The large park also has athletic fields for baseball, football, and soccer. (Gravano.)

A tranquil view across the Great South Bay is visible from Tanner Park. In Colonial times, residents from the northern shore of Long Island were drawn to the Copiague area to gather salt hay, which grew along the shore and was used to feed livestock. In the 21st century, the shoreline is cherished for its natural beauty and recreational enjoyment. (Rodi.)

BIBLIOGRAPHY

Bailey, Paul. *Historic Long Island in Pictures, Prose and Poetry.* Amityville, NY: Long Island Forum, 1956.

Bayles, Richard M. *History of Suffolk County, New York, with illustrations, portraits, and sketches of prominent families and individuals.* New York: W. W. Munsell and Company, 1882.

Dibbins, Elodie, Seth Purdy Jr., and Cecil H. Ruggles. *A Backward Glance.* Amityville, NY: Amityville Historical Society, 1980.

Eide, Elizabeth. *Copiague: Your Town and Mine.* Copiague, NY: Copiague Public Schools, 1971.

Huntington Historical Society. *Huntington-Babylon Town History.* Huntington, NY: Huntington Historical Society, 1937.

O'Connell, Walter G. *The "I" in Copiague Is Silent.* 1978.

Smith, Robert Mills. "A Brief History of the Town of Babylon." Babylon, NY: Town of Babylon, c. 1980.

Tooker, William Wallace. *The Indian Place-Names on Long Island and Islands Adjacent With Their Probable Significations.* New York: G. P. Putnam's Sons, 1911.

Towns of Huntington and Babylon, New York. *Huntington Town Records, Including Babylon, Long Island, NY, 1653–1688, Volume I.* Huntington, NY: Towns of Huntington and Babylon, 1887.

Vacca, Angelo. *Intimate Portraits of Old Copiague or A Boyhood Journey Through Old Copiague.* Copiague, NY: self-published, 2009.

INDEX

www.ingramcontent.com/pod-product-compliance
Lightning Source LLC
Chambersburg PA
CBHW080615110426
42813CB00006B/1516